THE MOUNTAIN BOY And THE FOREIGN AID CIRCUS

THE MOUNTAIN BOY
and
THE FOREIGN AID CIRCUS

CLAUDE W. BOBILLIER

VAJRA
BOOKS

Published & Distributed by

Vajra Books
Jyatha, Thamel, P.O. Box 21779, Kathmandu, Nepal
Tel.: 977-1-4220562, Fax: 977-1-4246536
e-mail: bidur_la@mos.com.np
www.vajrabooks.com.np

ISBN 978-9937-623-50-6

Printed in Nepal

CONTENTS

To my daughters Kate and Neen

PREFACE

There's a saying " Many are called but few are chosen." It's cited usually to refer to those who are engaged in some worthy mission or other. It indicates that not everyone is up to worthy missions. That's exactly how many feel about the 'Foreign Aid Circus'. Graham Hancock wrote about the few who were chosen in 'Lords of Poverty' but it was all too soon forgotten because he was 'teaching' us and it lacked what I would call 'a requisite of passion.' Even before Hancock, authors had chosen to deal with the topic through satire, but that's a long time ago. It needed a frank, frontal assault. This is probably that assault.

Dr. Bobillier, as they say in the crime stories, 'earns his bones' with this factual account of his work with foreign aid. He has had first-hand experience and not only with the scions of the helping classes but through his own life experiences and struggles from childhood in Switzerland to student hood and early life experiences in New Zealand. From his descriptions of his early years it is obvious that he was bound to have empathy with the disinherited of the earth. He could have remained in the boxed and defined environment of a conservative Swiss village. Needless to say he didn't, otherwise this book would have turned out quite differently.

The book covers a wide swathe of the global village and gives us insights into cultures which do not normally occur to international civil servants who are often too wrapped up in their own targets to stop and question whether these targets will serve the community they are intended for and finally make a difference to their lives and the lives of the children of the developing world. Targets, of course, are all very well but rather like the proverbial research recommendations all they seem to do is promote more of the same in an ever-ending circus of 'jobs for the boys', not to mention the girls! This is particularly true of education, Dr. Bobillier's field.

I first came across this author, and marked him away in the personal hard drive of my own grey matter, some years ago now when he sought language input (of the lighter variety) for his doctoral thesis. It was fortunate that all the talented young professionals of Nepal had not at that time been driven away by the Maoist conflict, internecine political squabbles and rank feudal cronyism and I was able to persuade an assistant editor to undertake the work with my guidance. We were both impressed, not only by the author's insight into the bottlenecks to delivering quality education to the young of Burkina Faso but by the obvious passion and commitment that shone through the pages.

Job done and we hardly met after that, or during for that matter – 'ships that pass in the night'. So many scholars and development workers/researchers have come into that category and as one ages more and more of them do tend to present themselves as a puzzle to be deciphered and placed in a particular learning file of one's life. Educationists know this only too well so perhaps Dr.Bobillier was surprised that I remembered him and in such detail.

I think those among you who wonder or who have ever wondered why much of foreign aid seems to have little or no impact at all should read this book. It tells of sincere advice unheeded by agencies who simply wish to pursue their own agenda, and governments too, why let them off the hook? We, who arrogantly believed ourselves 'the measure of all things', have mutely let a series of disasters go by and simply paid lip service to the term 'aid'. We have become, to borrow from a favourite series of young people's fiction, parsimonious, parseltongued creatures who grandstand our contributions to everything from genocide to earthquake relief!

I think Claude Bobillier is telling us that it's time to change, and I think he's right. His book gives you a selection of insights from several countries; and they are insights gleaned from first-hand experiences, and the way to find out whether you agree with his point of view or not is to read his book and compare it with experiences of your own.

Greta Rana,
Nepal, July 2015

ACKNOWLEDGEMENTS

Many family members and friends have, over the years, encouraged me to write about my professional experiences and life events, and they have, at times of weakening commitment and resolve, provided support and encouragement. Chief among them are one of my daughters, my brother, and some close friends.

In many ways, this book is the outcome of numerous – often intense – meetings and discussions with people I have been fortunate to work with. These people came from all walks of life and all sorts of backgrounds, and it was fascinating to hear and compare perspectives, frustrations, criticisms, aspirations, and hopes. There is no way I can sufficiently thank all the women and men, friends, students, professors, religious personalities, farmers, rickshaw pullers, government officers, researchers, heads of departments, traders, bureaucrats, and politicians; all of whom, in one way or another, offered me precious glimpses of their work, their country, and their own lives. I am deeply grateful to them all and sincerely hope that I have not distorted their views and contributions in the process of interpreting them.

INTRODUCTION

The decision to write about the events and experiences related here was precipitated by the gentle but steady encouragement and prodding, over many years, of family and friends. And I write primarily to share with them the multitude of extraordinary experiences and lessons learned over the course of a long, rich, and unusual career as an educational sociologist, consultant, and adviser. These experiences – so numerous, and so suffused with joy and pain – have had a deep and lasting impact upon me, and even to this day I feel the tug of a strange longing as I look back upon the years spent working among people alien to the privileges and comforts of life in the West.

Having worked over several decades in many different climates, with people of many different cultures; having travelled constantly and faced multitudes of values and attitudes; having been bewildered by the strangeness of language and aliens ways of life; now back in the West, I find myself longing for the simplicity and conviviality of people who – despite having to face daily the challenges of living in extreme poverty and deprivation – have not lost the essential humanity that Western societies, in their rush for material comforts and superficial wealth, seem to be so out of touch with.

The joy of a complete engagement in a worthy cause; the warmth and generosity of the people; the sense of having been useful, of having contributed to the betterment of someone else's life; at the end of the day, these are what contribute to the deep sense of satisfaction I often feel when I look back upon my life and work in the developing world. But, often, that joy and sense of satisfaction are tempered by the knowledge that much remains to be done, and the frustrations inherent in trying to make those in the indifferent West understand. If only they too could be witness to the sight of a village woman in Bangladesh confront so bravely not only poverty but also the ravages of natural disasters and man-made ones; and not once, and not twice; but year after year after year.

There is much potential in human beings everywhere, including in the poorest and the most illiterate societies. But everywhere such potential is being stifled by politicians, bureaucrats, and agents of change – especially foreign aid agents – who little understand ground realities and concerns. This book is, in many ways, an attempt to chronicle the successes and failures that I, over the course of a career that has taken me to thirty different countries on four different continents, have been witness to on the field and in the boardroom – where, alas, all too often, the most important decisions are still made.

Part I

THE EARLY YEARS

1

CHILDHOOD IN THE MOUNTAINS

I was born in 1939 in a modest working class family in a small and isolated village high up in the Alps, and I can still remember quite vividly the streets of the mountain village covered with thick snow for six months of the year; the seemingly endless winter nights of the early forties, cold and dark, and filled with the shrieking noise of American bombers passing overhead on their way to bomb Germany; the shutters covered to avoid the filtering of light; the infrequent visits of my father, who was forced to contribute to the defence of the homeland; the anxiety of my mother, who had to wash rich people's linen in order to make a meagre living and sustain the small family.

During, and immediately after, the Second World War, Switzerland displayed many of the characteristics of an underdeveloped country, and I grew up in a conservative and rigid society that esteemed material wealth and academic achievement over manual labour, and had little sympathy for people facing economic hardship. Consequently, the low socio-economic status of my family, together with the constant financial struggle of my poorly educated parents; the bullying and denigrating of teachers; the unsatisfactory academic results, especially when compared with those of my older, more academically inclined brother, who in the eyes of Mother and my teachers was the model that I ought to follow but obviously could not; the sheer uncertainty of life and the absence of hope of a decent future, all contributed to mould me into a somewhat confused and rebellious young man.

For years I suffered serious doubts about my worth as a person and over my own abilities, and I struggled with a lack of self-confidence and low self-esteem. It seemed that I was caught in a permanent but hopeless fight to overcome the frustration and rage of being nothing – a nobody in my own eyes. And this was further exacerbated by the fact I was constantly denied, as were my parents, the fair treatment and equality of opportunity that is the hallmark of an open society, which Switzerland was not really at that time. All this caused me to develop a hatred towards a society that treated its children not on the basis of potential or talent or merit, but on the basis of their father's occupation and social and financial status; and by the age of thirteen the seeds of rebellion had firmly been planted within me.

This, of course, would lead to all sorts of troubles at school and in the village itself. My behaviour became increasingly inappropriate – probably as a direct consequence of a subconscious attempt to compensate for my lack of self-esteem and feelings of inadequacy – and I took to fighting other boys, smoking, and bragging. Even ice-hockey – a sport I was rather good at – became solely a source of psychological compensation and a means of survival in a harsh world devoid of solidarity and compassion; a world where access to meaningful education was largely reserved for the well to do, and in which education itself constituted an efficient tool for perpetuating bourgeois values and preserving class interests through rigid social stratification, blatant injustices, and unequal treatment. And for me, as for many of my coevals, leaving the village, and its oppressive ways, seemed to be the only way to a better future elsewhere.

My father was a shy and soft-spoken loner – a man insufficiently understood and appreciated, even by his own wife and children. He worked as a cook in the village sanatorium; this until he lost his job, and with it what remained of his self-confidence. He would often take lonely bicycle rides in the nearby mountains, mostly to collect wild berries and to be closer to what was his best, and perhaps only true friend – nature. He also loved, and perhaps feared his wife, who only rarely returned his silent love, instead regularly deriding him, in front of his own children, for his weakness and lack of virility. Looking back, I find great sadness in the paradoxical fact that other in the extended family circle, along with our neighbours, knew and appreciated Father and his hidden inner qualities more than we – the members of his immediate family – ever did.

My mother was a strict woman, determined and hard working. She had never been given a chance to transcend her traumatized childhood and troubled roots and fulfil her many dreams – to travel and discover the wider world, to know a passionate and long-lasting love, to be free of financial hardship and live in comfort. For her, marrying my father – an equally destitute gentleman from the Italian part of the country, albeit refined and good-looking – had represented a step upward on the social ladder. She was the eldest of twelve siblings and spent her teens – when most girls go to school, play, and enjoy life – looking after and bringing up her sisters and brothers, two of whom died very young. Her own mother had little time to spare them, as she had to work hard to earn a living in the absence of her husband, who had died early of drink. Ill prepared for these very adult responsibilities that life had heaped upon her so early, she nonetheless carried out her duties bravely and earned the respect and gratitude of her younger brothers and sisters, for whom she had been almost a substitute mother.

In many ways, Ernest, my elder brother, suffered more than I did as a result of Mother's survival instincts, which had been sharpened all the more in the alien environment of her husband's home, where, among other things, she was forced to communicate in French, a language vastly different from her native German.

Growing up, the two of us could not have been more different. Perhaps, it was the difference in age, but Ernest always was the more emotionally stable, and this stability would continue on into adulthood and professional life. He also has always been a better family man and a more caring father. Moreover, throughout his very successful professional life been satisfied with his own society, its dominant values and ways, all of which he has seldom questioned and never rejected. This has often put him at odds against his younger brother and his constant questioning, criticisms, and partial rejection of Swiss bourgeois society with its self-centred individualism and excessive pursuit of material well being.

Or, perhaps, the difference in temperament was because of the fact that Mother treated us very differently. For example, she would speak to Ernest in German, while she only spoke to me in broken French. Also, Ernest was required to stay home and help Mother, while I was to go out, fight, and be a "real man". It was quite obvious that she had very different expectations of us.

A successful career and financial ease; a healthy dose of altruism and active human compassion, which have been translated into years of voluntary services on behalf of much less privileged individuals – mostly prisoners and destitute persons from developing countries; along with the crowning experience of being a grandfather several times over have largely contributed to transform old age into a sort of golden era for Ernest. For me, however, agitated and dissatisfied as I have always been, I have never stopped being a nomad, doubting, searching, and wanting to change the world. And this restlessness, especially when it comes to relationships with the other sex, I seem to have passed a little onto my daughters, and to this day I cannot but regret for having failed to provide the love and care that is so vital for girls to mature into fulfilled women.

One of the consequences of the difference in temperament was that while life at school was a relatively happy and fulfilling experience for Ernest, it was not the same for me. And this was made worse by Ernest's successes – which though often a source of pride for me were also a source of frustration – and his being regarded as a "model" brother. This frustration would last well into adulthood, up until when I received my doctorate – something that Ernest had not achieved, despite the ease with which he accomplished his intellectual pursuits.

Formal schools in Swiss mountain villages in the fifties were not the ideal places to acquire a fulfilling all-round education that would prove useful in professional life, and I was subjected to a useless, discipline-centred approach that, unfortunately, so many children around the world still have to suffer. Rote-learning and the regurgitation of utterly useless information was the norm; added to which an over-emphasis on academic success and competition further contributed to the stifling the children's creative and learning instincts and potential for intellectual growth.

Further, physical and verbal violence were accepted practices in many of the so-called difficult schools – schools with large populations of working class and foreign children, who often faced learning difficulties. Whereas Ernest received smiles and praise from the teachers, I received the opposite – denigration: "You will not even find a job as a street cleaner," I remember a teacher saying to me. All this added to my growing lack of self-confidence and sense of shame and inadequacy. As a result, I detested school, and not only because I felt belittled and persecuted but because even then I could understand how the school and the teachers were failing in their duty to instil in me and the other children the sense of joy of discovery and learning that is so important to the growth of young minds. And when I look back I can see how easily I could have fallen into delinquency and become a social reject. However, the rage and resentment inside my heart became the engines not of crime, but of a profound and lasting desire to contribute to change society, especially the education sector; and to this day education of the underprivileged, the poor, and the socially oppressed remain my professional passions.

However, life was not completely filled with difficulties alone. There was, of course, the lakes and the rivers and the mountains, most of which I discovered with my father on our berry-gathering expeditions. It is from him that I inherited my deep love for the same and, also, for nature in general. From him, also, as from my mother and a few significant others, I inherited a strong commitment to essential values, such as respect for others regardless of status, gender, and race; the importance of fairness and equality; and the necessity of hard work and perseverance. I also developed a dislike for conformity, traditions, authority, and the blind adherence to beliefs. Even early in life I had a sense of the existence of some sort of ultimate truth that went beyond traditions; beyond accepted social norms; beyond the hypocritical masks and pretences of "normal" society; and, above all, beyond words. Exploring this would ultimately lead me to staying three months in a Hindu monastery in South India, where I would realize that, ultimately, human beings long for spirituality and a means to transcend the meaninglessness and lack of fulfilment of ordinary life. I have also felt always a powerful disgust towards all forms of discrimination, especially racial discrimination; an aversion to vulgarity, bragging, excessive self-centredness, and any form of cruelty, especially the self-serving corruption and pomposity of governing elites. All this has contributed to an uncompromising sense of fairness, which, over the course of the many years that I have worked abroad, has led to situations where I have had to face everything from deportation to death threats.

2

TOWARDS ADULTHOOD

Following the end of the war and the subsequent transformation of the village from a place of convalescence into a tourist destination, my father, at the age of fifty-six, lost his job and was forced to look for another source of income. This meant moving away from our small and isolated mountain community to the distant valley below – to a new world frightening in its sophistication to my unprepared parents. For me, of course, this was an altogether more positive experience, as living in a town meant a lifestyle more in keeping with the wants of an adolescent in the process of discovering his emerging sexuality.

A post-office job meant that I now had money of my own and was able – with the help of my parents – to purchase a car. And even though it was only a ramshackle Simca, it meant the world to me and to my parents, who had hardly had the opportunity to ride in one before. Working as a humble clerk – one of the few jobs then available to me with my meagre qualifications and low social status – however, left me deeply unsatisfied. For me – who longed for a life of action, travel, and encounters with other cultures, people, and ways of life – spending my days sitting in a small office seemed to be a complete waste of time, and, so, when the opportunity arrived, at the age of nineteen, I joined the army.

As is the case the world over with many a poor and under-educated boy, the army would be one of the most positive experiences of my life. Confused, naive, and searching for a raison d'être, I found in the army a sense of purpose, an identity, and camaraderie that would do much to boost my fragile self-confidence. However, the honeymoon did not last long, and much to Mother's disappointment – she had seen my joining the army as a sign of virility missing from the rest of the male members of the family – I was thrown out of the army after eight months, after openly voicing my disagreement regarding the treatment of terrified recruits by some idiotic officers.

My own lack of direction, both emotional and professional, and my growing disenchantment with the Swiss way of life – a stifling, monotonous, and unduly materialistic existence that offered no attractions to an unskilled and under-educated young man – led me to seek out newer horizons, and when the opportunity to venture abroad arrived I accepted it with more than a little gladness. My brother had arranged a job for me as a ski instructor in New Zealand, which I accepted at once, little knowing how the decision would completely change the course of my life.

The decision was not easy to take for my parents. Four years earlier, in 1957, Ernest had decided to move to New Zealand, whose very name terrified Mother, who was convinced that cannibals waited for her son there, at the end of the world. Now, four years later, to the grief of my parents, there I was, following my brother's lead. Neither one of us would ever see our parents again.

I left in June 1961 by train, still only a naive twenty-two year old, devastated at the thought of leaving my parents. The parting was extremely painful, and as I looked at Mother waving from the kitchen window and quietly sobbing, I was vaguely conscious of the fact that it was the last time I would be seeing her. And her expression as she waved to me has never quite left me, and to this day it continues to guide me.

And it was much the same with Father, standing next to the little white Renault, a car in which they were both to die a year and a half later. I had urged them to buy the car, as it would at least allow them to visit friends and relatives once I left home....

From Egypt, I sailed for New Zealand on an old Dutch ship – the Olden Barnevelt – filled with European migrants in search of work and a better life. Life on the ship was a completely new experience, and quite pleasant at that. I shared a primitive and stifling cabin with six other young migrants from six different countries, an experience that was at once fun and challenging, especially as I had never before left Switzerland and had no experience of other cultures. And it was on the rickety boat that I fell in love for the second time in my life.

The first time had been when I was nineteen and had fallen head over heels in love with Marianne – a delightfully feminine and bright German girl. In so doing I'd first experienced the delights, the torments, and the upheavals of love. And Marianne, more than any other, gave me glimpses into the unfathomable depths of the female soul and its endless possibilities. And Marikje, the Dutch student on the ship, she contributed to this as well, so that I grew to be fascinated by the mystery that is womanhood in all its aspects; a fascination that continues to this day, and that grew into amazement after having witnessed the resiliency, the courage, and the selflessness in women in places as diverse as Bangladesh, the Philippines, Cambodia, and parts of Africa.

We arrived in New Zealand early in the morning on a grey and windy mid-winter day. I stood on the top deck of the ship, searching in the vast crowd on the waterfront for my brother, whom I had not seen for five years. Suddenly, to my immense relief, I caught sight of him. He was standing in the midst of the vast crowd, an elegant and beautiful lady standing next to him. She was Anna, the only wife that stable Ernest has ever had, and to this day, my very close friend and confidante. She had grown up in Soviet occupied Hungary, and the traumas she had to face there, along with those that she faced as a refugee fleeing the Soviets, had moulded her into a caring and loving person whose role in aiding my daughter has left me eternally indebted to her.

3

A NEW BEGINNING

The warm welcome with which I was received did much to help me settle down quickly in New Zealand, a country I grew fond of immediately, and one that to this day continues to charm me. There was the natural beauty; the unpolluted spaces and endless white beaches; the forests, dense and diverse; the endless green meadows ... Added to that, I found a society completely different from Swiss society. Not only were the two countries antipodes of each other geographically but they were similarly antipodean in their collective mentalities, in their modes of thinking, and in their approach to social structures and functioning. On the one hand was New Zealand, a young society characterized by a refreshingly daring and pioneering spirit; widespread optimism; pragmatism; social flexibility; and a deep sense of fairness, meritoriousness, respect, and equality; while, on the other, there was the old, conservative and elitist Switzerland, clinging to its ancient traditions and norms, social discrimination and stratification, and counterproductive class privileges based on social origin rather than individual merit.

Shortly after my arrival in Wellington, I left for the volcanic mountains of the North, where the job that Ernest had found for me was waiting at the Château, a budding winter resort at the foot of Mount

Ruapehu, an active volcano. However, when I got there there was not a trace of snow on the rocky and treeless slopes. In the absence of work, all there was to do for me and my fellow ski instructors – a bunch of freshly arrived European men from Austria and Switzerland, naive and uneducated – was to chase after and chat up young Kiwi girls, many of whom treated us like demi-gods; share inane jokes; and make small talk. This was not exactly what I'd prepared myself for, and I was more than a little disappointed. However, there was consolation in the fact that it was there that I met Manfred, a young German, who would become one of my very best friends – in fact, unknown to us then, I would be the best man at his wedding to Judith – a local lady – a few years later.

When the snow finally arrived it brought with it the Maori farm-based prisoners, whose job it was to shovel the snow and prepare paths and slopes in preparation for the skiers just discovering the new winter sport. Meeting and interacting with Maoris was a revelation to me. These huge, brown, always smiling people – certainly no cannibals as Mother had feared! – were the first people from a "different" race that I had met, and I was quite amazed by their friendliness and could not understand how such charming creatures were in prison. My later encounters with them largely confirmed my feelings towards them, and I would go on, at university, to study their culture and develop much admiration for it. Emphasizing the harmony of the collective over the individual's separate identity, it stood quite in contrast with the blinkered European vision that even now clings to history and culture as illusory sources of security and individual identity.

Politicians and bureaucrats in New Zealand at the time seemed to have genuinely felt that their essential duty was to serve the people rather than profit from, and take advantage of, the system. Merit and performance were then the main yardsticks by which individuals were judged; the education system was regularly reviewed, and its purpose, role, objectives and strategies were reshaped and realigned as necessary. By then New Zealand, with its generous welfare state, concern for human rights (including women's rights – it was the first country to grant women the right to vote), and the fair treatment of its dominant minorities – the Maoris, had become the social laboratory of the world, and in many ways, the antithesis of Switzerland.

I had initially planned to stay six months; I ended up living there for eleven years.

Over the next few years I worked on several unskilled jobs. Following my stint as a ski instructor and part time chairlift boy, I worked as a painter on a construction site; a farm hand building fences on isolated hills on the South Island; a watchman at a city museum; and, finally, as a waiter in several posh restaurants and night clubs. The waiting jobs allowed me to save enough for me to pursue my studies at university at the same time and were also were rich sources of experience and learning, in that they allowed me to see the inherent worth of each and every occupation, and how stratifying them according to a value system largely developed by the rich and educated minorities is harmful not only to individuals but society at large.

The waiting work was exhausting, especially as I was a student at the same time, but it was also fun and socially and financially rewarding. I loved meeting people, and my efficiency and politeness, along with my French accent and my reasonably good looks, earned the appreciation of colleagues, bosses, and clients alike, and I was frequently rewarded with generous tips. One day I was asked to serve a very special and important guest. A rather faded old lady and her entourage soon turned up for lunch and were seated at the beautifully decorated table. She was Vivian Leigh, the actress from "Gone with the Wind". She was very charming, and when I was introduced as her waiter, she smiled at me and said, "Hello, young man." Later, as a reward for my services, I was invited to sit down at her table and shown hundreds of photos of Clark Gable and herself. She was young and extremely beautiful in the pictures, and I could not but enthusiastically commended her on the same. As reward I received a tip so big that it left both me and my boss, Madame Louise – a large and loud and rather matronly lady from Normandy – dazed. However, the experience left me with a sense of sadness, as I'd witnessed first hand how this old and fragile lady could not reconcile herself to the fact that her once famous beauty had long faded and that she was no longer the celebrity whom the world had once worshipped.

The money from the waiting job, besides enabling me to pay for my studies, also allowed me to support my parents financially. This was especially important as their earnings were barely sufficient to make ends meet. Moreover, sending the money helped ease my conscience just a little of the guilt I felt over my leaving home for New Zealand.

Wellington in the early sixties, was an easy going, open and tolerant city, and especially keen to absorb European ways, from skiing to food and wine. For a young man like myself, always yearning for new experiences, it was the ideal place to be. There was lots of time on hand to go to the beach, parties, and dances. My work, along with the fact that I attended college, meant that I was offered plenty of opportunities to meet people, especially young women; to flirt and to fall in love all too easily and frequently. By then, of course, I had developed a great deal of interest in the other sex and took full advantage of my age and my French accent – which, surprisingly even to myself, had proved an unbelievable asset when it came to young women. I was rarely alone, and seduction quickly became an exciting game, but one that quickly turned empty and cruel and lasted, unfortunately, far too long.

4

GRIEF

Late on a Sunday morning on November 24, 1962, I was woken up by a ring at the front door. I crawled out of bed; I had spent the night at work at the Zodiac – an elegant night club in Wellington where I worked every Saturday night – and was exhausted. At the time I was still living with my brother and sister-in-law, but they were out that weekend. I opened the door to find a yellow envelope on the floor. Opening it, I read the telegram from my uncle addressed to Ernest and me. It was in French: "Parents décédés," it said; "rentrez immédiatement." My parents were dead and my uncle had asked us to return at once.

From that moment on my life took a drastic turn and became largely unbearable for the next three years. The events of that day would largely dictate the subsequent course of my life, which would become a pursuit of some sort of atonement. In death my parents became far more significant than they had ever been alive. For the first time in my short life I discovered the meaning of loneliness and isolation, and I would not allow even my brother to share that overbearing pain and hopelessness. It seemed as if guilt and despair had taken completely over my heart and soul.

I had not been a caring enough son during my wasteful and self-centred adolescence, and what about the suffering I had inflicted upon my parents by migrating to the ends of the earth? And to all that there was the fact that I felt partially responsible for their death. What could I do to atone or repent? To move on with my own life and be free once and for all of the vicious cycle of guilt, emotional turmoil, and shame? My desire to assist my parents to settle down into a more or less comfortable retirement had been an important motivating factor in my going abroad. The fact that this wish had been so brutally frustrated by death quickly became a source of despair and for three long years I had horrible nightmares, cried frequently, and may even have been close to madness at times.

I would learn later that the accident had happened on a perfectly straight road not far from where they lived and that Mother – still learning to drive – had been at the wheel. She had swerved to avoid a cyclist and had instead crashed headlong into a large car coming from the opposite direction. Father died instantly, while Mother survived the accident only to die in hospital. Mother's last words, upon realizing that her husband was dead, was, "Mon Dieu, qu'est-ce que j'ai fait?" (My God, what have I done?). I went to the scene of the crash a few weeks after I arrived in Switzerland and found, on the grass next to the road, some teeth, but I've never been able to find out if they were my parents'.

I had taught my mother the rudiments of driving, even after I had realized that she was far too old and too nervous of temperament to drive. Also, it was I who had encouraged them to purchase the car, as it would have meant they would have been able to visit family and friends after I'd left. All this, of course, only served to intensify my sense of guilt and shame.

Later, my former village pastor suggested I channel and redirect my guilt into something more constructive and useful – humanitarian work in developing countries. And that is what I decided to do when my attempt to become a Hindu monk in South India had failed. At that time, however, I wanted to give it all up and go and become a fisherman in India. I believed that I would find meaning there, and forgiveness. I look back now and realize that all this was nothing more than a sort of self-flagellation for largely imaginary sins. I also understand now that my extreme reactions were not motivated by self-pity alone, but also by genuine grief at the loss of my parents and for their life too – they had never known a fulfilling and comfortable life, but only one of constant struggles and few joys.

The news left our little family stunned and almost unable to cope with the demands of daily life, and it was only the extraordinary support of our Kiwi friends – who took upon themselves to look after us, to shop, cook, etc. – that allowed us to survive the ordeal. The extraordinarily supportive reaction of these friends is something that I have never forgotten, and in my moments of doubt – and there are many – I still look upon such precious acts of friendship and am hopeful again for the world.

The fact that Anna was pregnant at the time meant that Ernest could not travel and it was decided that I would travel to Europe alone at a later date to take care of our parents' affairs. At that time the only way to travel to Europe from the Antipodes was by ship, and as Swiss law did not permit the keeping of dead bodies beyond three days, there was no point in hurrying back. Ernest was distraught over the fact that he could not travel with me and help me with the difficult tasks that awaited me.

On a warm summer morning in late January, 1963, I embarked for Athens on the Wilhelm Ruis, another Old Dutch ship. Other than the fact that my lower deck cabin – which cost ninety two British pounds – was crowded with smoking migrants returning home, I have little recollection of the six week journey; so intense was my sense of hopelessness and dread of the prospect of having to open the door of the empty flat and deal with my parents' personal affairs. Neither can I remember anything of my arrival in Athens in the middle of the winter and the subsequent train trip to Switzerland.

I arrived in Lausanne, on 6 March, 1963, and was met at the station by my brother's best friend. I rested at his house for a few days and then travelled on his scooter to the village where my parents had spent their final days.

I entered the small sealed flat and the first thing I noticed was its usual tidiness, even after the police had visited it three months earlier. I saw the little pieces of paper on which Mother had written down instructions to Father regarding daily chores and personal hygiene and pinned them in various places. It only served to heighten further my sense of loss and despair. Realizing that I could not go through the ordeal by myself, I appealed for help, and a cousin from a nearby city came and stayed with me for a few days. Her words and presence did much to help me gather myself up, and though she and I have had our differences over the years, I always remember this act of hers with the utmost gratitude. Moreover, it was her father – my uncle – that had overseen affairs in the aftermath of the accident, and he had taken care of all the details extremely well, and it was he that had sent us the fateful telegram.

I sorted out my parents' possessions and readied them for distribution among family members. However, the bickering of Mother's three sisters over those three heaps of miserable belongings was such a distressing scene that it haunts me to this day. After ten days, having completed all of my duties, I had only one thought in mind: to leave the hated land as soon as possible. But where was I to go and to whom?

In March I returned to the village of my birth, and then journeyed to Zurich – where I'd worked as a postal clerk in the fifties – to seek the comfort of old friends, including Nellie, my old English teacher, who would become a surrogate mother to me; and Sylvia, the pretty European roller skating champion; and Selvarajan, my old yoga teacher. It was Selvarajan who suggested that I travel to India, and it was thanks to him that I was accepted at the Ramakrishna Mission.

5

ESCAPE TO INDIA

I arrived in Madras (now Chennai) in the summer of 1963 and immediately began life as a sannyasin (Hindu monk) at the Ramakrishna Mission, a religious charity focused on the study and practical application of the Bhagavad Gita – which was Mahatma Gandhi's guiding force in successful non-violent struggle for India's independence – and serving the poorest of the poor across India. Ramakrishna – a nineteenth century saint, who reached the enlightened state called nirvana at the end of his life, and Vivekananda – his brilliant disciple – preached and assiduously practised intensive meditation while actively spreading the Gita's stirring message and assisting countless numbers of downtrodden people.

For a young Westerner – I was only twenty-four at the time – arriving in India was quite an experience, and one that I found extremely difficult to cope with. The combination of extreme heat and humidity; the strange smells; dirt; poverty; as well as the masses of staring brown people at first terrified and repelled me to the extent that a few hours after arriving in India I was ready to board the next plane back to Europe. However, the first shock did not last long, and I quickly discovered at the monastery a strange but deeply moving world.

Barely speaking any English, let alone the local language, and lost in the complexities of Hindu mysticism and culture, I, nonetheless, made every effort to settle down and assimilate with the other sannyasins. They were all Indian, well educated and secure in their chosen vocation; in their conviction to give up the materialistic and superficial world outside the monastery; and in their decision to free themselves from attachment to family and friends. The goodness of their hearts, their tolerance and patience, along with the kindness of the head monk – Swami Kailashananda – and other senior monks helped me immensely. Never had I experienced such warmth, compassion, and selflessness. I was deeply touched, and all the kindness helped me get on the road to emotional and psychological recovery.

However, I struggled immensely with the food – usually rice and bananas served on banana leaves, and provided by devotees from Madras – and the daily cycle of prayers, long periods of silent meditation, monastery duties, and social work at the dispensary attached to the monastery. Moreover, I suffered from a serious lack of sleep because of the heat, humidity and the mosquitoes. Taking into account my difficulties, the monastery authorities were prepared to bend the strict rules that govern Ramakrishna missions everywhere, and once a week I was allowed to eat outside the monastery, and was also given permission to turn up at the morning prayer at six in the morning instead of four. Moreover, when it came to me, other rules too were bent or only applied very leniently, and I began to realize that the monastic life was not for me and that I was better off looking for another vocation.

I left the monastery and the friendship of my companions after less than three months. However, fifty years later, the experience remains with me, along with Swami Kailashananda's words upon my departure. "You have had the privilege of living among us," he said; "surrounded by love and spirituality. We hope that you have gained from this experience and further developed your own humanity. Now you do have some duties towards your fellow men in the West, who too are searching, and often in the dark. Therefore, go and share with them the experiences and the benefits you may have gathered here." I did not know how to respond to his words but with tears, and set out to return to the world – to the banalities of modern city life in the West, with its superficiality and its mundane preoccupations, and I found the experience of returning as much of a culture shock as India had initially been.

I had made much progress emotionally and psychologically, and that was due entirely to the nurturing care that my fellow sannyasins, a rare and beautiful breed of men. Years later, in the vast emptiness of the deserts of West Africa, I worked and briefly lived with a similarly exceptional breed of men: The White Fathers, a religious order whose adherents devote their lives completely to the poor and needy.

It has always been, and still is, a puzzle to me – the fact that such inner beauty and nobility of spirit are almost always found outside the West, in places like India, Nepal, Bangladesh, Cambodia and Africa. For many years now I have been convinced that that these cultures all have in common the fact that they emphasize the solidarity of the whole over the individual and his profits; that they have great respect for their elders as valuable sources of experiences, knowledge, and wisdom; and also for nature; and that they treat strangers with kindness and respect. And it is this that enables these people – some of whom come from the poorest communities on Earth – to enjoy life despite their hardships. And to this day I wonder why we in the West have never bothered to learn the lessons that these people may have to teach us. What reason could we have in refusing to learn from them, other than arrogance?

The Ramakrishna Mission experience, apart from ensuring a lifelong fascination and attraction towards India, also played a crucial role in my life, in that it compelled me to dedicate my life to humanitarian work.

6

RETURN TO NEW ZEALAND

Not wanting to return to Europe, the only feasible option for me was to return to New Zealand, and I quite looked forward to the prospect, as it seemed to me that I had sampled but little of the possibilities of life Down Under.

I took seriously the head monk's final words to me, but how was I share those precious gifts with my fellow Europeans? I stuck, for some time at least, to some of the practices I'd learned at the monastery – sleeping on a hard board; avoiding the company of women; living in a simple and bare environment; and being content with just the basic necessities of life and not indulging in excesses, both physical and emotional. Some of these have remained with me until today, but many didn't, especially the one that required one to avoid the company of women, which was rapidly discarded as I encountered some delightful young women in Wellington and my libido gained the upper hand in the battle with my austerities.

I went back to university and began to pursue studies that would prepare me for my subsequent involvement in developing countries, including India. Sociology and education, had begun to fascinate me, as I loved learning new things about different countries and their problems. In addition to these, I was also attracted to geography, history, anthropology, and psychology. It seemed to me that the world's problems could at least partially be resolved through a wise application of the knowledge acquired through the study of these disciplines.

At university I met a number of people who were to have a lasting effect on my life. The first of these was George Parkyn and his family. One Sunday evening I received a call from a soft spoken gentleman who told me that he had heard about me from university friends and that he wanted to know if I would be interested in having conversations in French with him and his family every Sunday over a meal; it was so as to enable the family to practise their French. George Parkyn was the head of the educational research division of the Ministry of Education; a renowned writer; and, later, would be a distinguished visiting professor at Stanford and London University. I was quite intimidated, but I accepted the invitation and was suddenly thrust into the highest academic circles in the land. More importantly, though, it would mark the beginning of a lifelong and very rewarding friendship with a highly cultivated yet modest Kiwi family.

There was also Jim Robb, foremost among the many professors whose capacity to assist struggling students earned my unequivocal respect. A shy and exquisitely polite gentleman, Jim, made sociology – especially educational sociology – so appealing to me that I would take it up as my life's vocation.

Both of the men shared, along with the many other Kiwis who would make an impression on me then, character traits that I found especially attractive – modesty, kindness, a sense of humour, warmth, and genuine concern for others.

And then there was Susanne. I met her in 1963, when I was still trying to live as a monk amid the many temptations of a Western city, all the while struggling to cope with the burden of my studies. She and I were both enrolled for a class in Education taught by Dr. Bailey, a charming old professor, and I still remember very clearly how she would turn back towards me from her bench a few rows down from mine. Flattered by the interest, I finally plucked up the courage to speak to her. Of course, I was still involved in practising the things I'd learnt at the Ramakrishna Mission and a part of me feared what she as a woman represented – a potential loss of vital energy better utilized for spiritual ends!

Susanne opened the doors to a new world for me – the world of share brokers and lawyers; the world of high finance, where old men clung still to Victorian glories. I was impressed, although I identified little with it. I had by then become rather obsessed by India and strongly felt the need to go back there and work for the uplifting of the poor. I tried to convince Susanne to accompany me, and in the end she agreed, to the extent that she was ready to invest a significant amount of her own money in the endeavour. And in so doing she conquered me completely and our destinies were marked by a common seal.

I wasn't doing very well at university; in fact, I'd failed my first year, and this had led me to question my intelligence and abilities. Susanne was instrumental in preventing me from slipping further. It was not stupidity that was my problem, she pointed out; rather, it was the complete lack of method in my approach to my studies. She was correct, and once I had rectified that, studying became easier for me and quickly obtained a BA, followed by a BA Honours, and later, an MA and a PhD.

Not surprisingly, my studies were focused, as much as possible, on issues that were, and still are, of deep concern to me – juvenile delinquency and poverty and the role of education in reducing it. My MA dissertation focused on truancy in New Zealand, while my doctorate focused on popular participation in education in the African Sahel.

It was during this time that Susanne and I met a rather extraordinary man, a brilliant student named Fafa. He was from Gambia and was altogether unique. He had arrived on a scholarship to study law and must have been the first black African person to set foot on New Zealand soil. All those who met Fafa were fascinated by the man; he had striking features, was tall and handsome, with a serene and noble face that immediately commanded respect; and added to that, he had an imposing aristocratic bearing. However, the most striking thing about him was his academic brilliance and his ease with words – he was a real poet in the

African oral tradition. I was enthralled by the man and his seemingly limitless capacities, his charm, his eloquence. In many ways, Fafa was then much like Barack Obama is today. Most women were seduced by Fafa on first sight, and men were left fascinated and speechless.

Fafa became a close friend of mine, partly because of my boundless admiration for all facets of the man. Fafa called me brother and treated me with genuine affection, probably feeling rather sorry for my academic struggles. However, two years later, Fafa left New Zealand in a hurry – he had been accused by the university authorities of cheating twice at the end of the year's examinations; an accusation Fafa vehemently denied, and I, in my blind devotion to the man, saw only racism in the allegations and supported him throughout. Prior to his departure, though, Fafa admitted to me that he had indeed cheated and that he had lied to all, including me – his trusting and naive white brother. Incredulous, I asked him why – why cheat when he was the best by a long margin? The answer was dry and brutal: "Take a look at this very black skin of mine, brother. Don't you know that this is the skin of slaves and that you and the likes of you have been the enslavers? To beat you all at your own game is my pleasure and belated revenge on your race; to make sure that the revenge is complete, yes I do at times cheat to ensure ultimate success." And in this one incident I have always seen a disturbing illustration of what colonialism has done to the self-confidence and dignity of Africans.

Twenty years later Fafa would re-emerge in my life. I was studying for my PhD at the Institute of Education, London University, and a fellow student from Gambia had led me back to him. He had completed his education in England and had become, much to my surprise, Gambia's attorney general. I had called him from Senegal, and he asked me to visit him immediately so as to celebrate our reconnecting again after so many years. The next day, in Banjul, the dusty capital of poverty stricken Gambia, I was received at the airport as a VIP and chauffeur-driven to the attorney general's office in the centre of the city. That night he hosted, in my honour, in a restaurant overlooking the sea, a dinner that felt almost like a state dinner. Fafa presided over the festivities with characteristic ease and humour, and seated me at the head of an imposing table filled with many dignitaries – on my left was seated Tolbert, the brother of Liberia's former president; on the right, a gentleman who happened to be the former vice-president of Sierra Leone; both charming and interesting men, their charm belying the ruthlessness with which they had ruled over their people. Both men had fled their respective countries following coups and had taken up asylum in Gambia, where Fafa provided them shelter, probably in the hope that they would return the favour when the time came and he too was kicked out of his country, which did happen quite soon after.

Two days later, late in the evening Fafa called me and ordered me to be ready for dinner with some ladies. I pointed out to him that it was already eleven at night, but Fafa would not listen; instead, he repeated that he would be at my hotel in ten minutes. Later, he pointed out to me that as my older African brother he had the traditional duty of finding a new wife for me, and that it was quite unhealthy for a fellow like me to live alone. The young lady came and went. She was 17 and very beautiful, but we did not speak a single word.

The last time I heard of Fafa, the regime had just been replaced by an incompetent military regime, and he was under house arrest in Gambia for not having paid his taxes. I was in Tanzania when I received a phone call from Fafa asking me if I was still his young white brother. When I answered yes, he went on to ask me for a loan of 50,000 British pounds to pay for his release. Of course, I – much to Fafa's surprise – was in no position to help.

Susanne and I got married in 1965. After a brief honeymoon in Fiji, we left for Europe and a new life away from what Susanne saw as the stifling conservatism of her family. By the winter of 1967, we had settled into a simple flat by Lake Zurich. We were prepared to take on Switzerland!

In hindsight, we rushed into the whole thing rather blindly. We were both unprepared for it and in the end the marriage lasted only seven years.

7

RETURN TO SWITZERLAND

In the years following the end of the Second World War, Switzerland – which had been spared the war for reasons that were neither obvious nor glorious (as would be revealed later) – began to establish a solid economic base, and by the time I returned, the country had developed into one of the most prosperous on Earth, with an economy that was the envy of much of the world.

Finding a job in the winter of 1967, then, did not prove a particularly difficult task; after all, I had recognized university qualifications and very good command of three languages. Settling down, however, proved a little more difficult. I had left the country six years earlier feeling a sense of disgust, and though I was now a different man, and the country too had changed much, I found still something of the collective mentality of the old country – the smugness, self-satisfaction, and absurd sense of superiority. All this I abhorred, especially after the experience of New Zealand and its freedom and friendliness. At the age of twenty-eight, I for the first time of his life entered the murky corporate world, working initially for a large Swiss bank and, later, for a powerful foreign oil company as a socio-economic researcher. The work was interesting, challenging, and the pay always decent; however, I never felt at ease in the corporate world and could never share its values. The overwhelming focus of productivity and profits over all other considerations, including the possible impact on humans and the environment, often left me appalled. And added to that was the fear of authority and servility, the psychological brutality, and lack of human sensitivity of some corporate bosses; and the blind acceptance on the part of most employees of their superiors' decisions; all far removed from the world I knew in India and New Zealand.

I left after two years, convinced more than ever that my vocation lay elsewhere.

A few months later our daughter, Olga, was born. Plump and beautiful, she added a sense freshness to our lives. The times were particularly turbulent and exciting – universities in California and Europe were exploding with student protests against the stifling ways and amoral and unfair practices of Western societies. These were the days of Herbert Marcuse and his One Dimensional Man; of Angela Davis and the Black Panthers in America; of Alexander Dubcek's Prague Spring, which was crushed by Soviet tanks. In America, Robert Kennedy had been murdered, and so had Martin Luther King, and a year later, in the summer of 1969, even as the Vietnam War intensified, Neil Armstrong, would step on the moon. It seemed as if Olga had been born on the cusp of history.

She was born in a small lake side maternity on August 14, 1968. I had taken an active part in the preparation for her arrival, but nothing could prepare me for the overwhelming emotions I felt upon her birth, and I will never forget Susanne's radiant face and the intensity of her eyes at the moment of parturition.

Apart from reading good old Doctor Spock and listening to the advice of friends and family, we had prepared little for the baby. Olga's arrival, as is sometimes the case with married couples, instead of uniting us served to accentuate our differences, especially regarding responsibilities and expectations. I felt increasingly let down by Susanne and resented the fact – as I perceived it then – that she was not doing her fair share of the household work, and this – a result of my Swiss upbringing – Susanne took for pettiness on my part. There were other differences too, brought about by our different cultural backgrounds and psychological make-up, and all of them contributed to the growing misunderstanding and tension between us.

A year later Susanne left for London, but a few months later we were back together, and we decided to move back to New Zealand and begin anew.

8

ALTRUISM

About the time of Olga's birth, I met again Appadurai Aaron, a retired Indian gentleman who had been a professor at Chicago University and had taught for over thirty years. He would become my mentor, guide, and one of my most beloved friends, and I saw him more as a saint than a man. I had met Padre – as he was popularly known – for the first time two years earlier in New Zealand in somewhat strange circumstances. Prior to my leaving for India to become a monk, Selvarajan – my yoga teacher in Switzerland – had given me his uncle's address and instructed me to go to him should I fail as a monk; the uncle was heavily involved in the development and support of five extremely poor and isolated villages in Tamil Nadu, the Southern Indian state. However, I had not met him in India, but one day I attended at the university a deeply moving lecture on rural poverty in India. The lecturer's name seemed very familiar, and, sure enough, when I looked it up in my address book at home, it turned out to be the same man. I called the university at once and ended up meeting Padre for the first time close to midnight.

When I met him in Switzerland, he asked me if I'd be willing, when required, to assist him with his work in India. He was growing old and blind, and I felt honoured that he should have asked me to be a part of his noble and selfless endeavour. Padre himself had taken up the initiative as a tribute to his late wife, Ranji, and the project was named Ranji Aaron Memorial Project. It was, as Padre himself put it, the handkerchief with which he could wipe his tears after her sudden death in the Swiss Alps.

Padre's call came six years later, in 1974. He sent a brief cable asking me to come to his assistance – insufficient rains had brought about a famine-like situation in the five villages. At the time I was working as a school teacher in New Zealand, and with two daughters to raise, my finances were severely stretched. I could not afford the plane ticket to India. I was desperate as there was nothing more I wanted to do than travel to India and fulfil my promise to Padre.

My class was composed mainly of children from working class backgrounds and broken families, full of life and energy, but struggling with academic pursuits; as such they were considered "difficult" and "problematic". In many ways they reminded me of my younger self, and I felt a great affinity for them and believed that they could – with the proper support and in the proper environment – flourish and prove their worth.

One day, at the beginning of class, a fifteen year old girl walked up to me and asked me why I'd been reading the same piece of paper over and over again for the last few days. Slightly embarrassed, I told her that it was nothing; however, she was insistent, and so I showed her the cable and explained to her my predicament. She read the cable silently and returned to her seat without saying a word. A week later she walked up to me before class and handed me a rather thick envelope. I opened the envelope – there was over seven hundred dollars there along with a note signed by all twenty-three students. It said: "Sir, now please go to India and assist your old friend Padre and these starving Indians in their villages ..."

I was left stunned and speechless. Tears streaming down my face I sat down on my chair. Where had they got the money from, I asked them, when I had recovered my composure a little. They had worked for it after school – washing dishes and cars, mowing lawns, baby-sitting.... I was overwhelmed and had to retreat to my office lest they saw me cry. This was one of the most beautiful gestures I have witnessed, and the lesson that these "difficult" children taught me will never be forgotten.

The next day, I swung into action. Talk shows, TV appearances, meetings at Rotary and Lion clubs followed each other rapidly over the next two weeks as I attempted to raise funds for the villages. The response was overwhelming, and it was not only the generosity of individual citizens that moved me, but the reaction of the authorities as well. Just before leaving for India, I received a call from the Prime Minister's Office. It was his assistant – apparently the PM had seen me on television and had instructed his office to deposit two thousand dollars with the New Zealand Embassy in Delhi for me to collect on behalf of Padre and the five villages. Thanks to the generosity of many – including quite a few in Switzerland – substantial funds were collected to feed the villagers and set the project on a sounder footing.

Some time later, Padre died peacefully in his own village, among his own people. Shortly before his death, on his last trip to Europe, he had met Ernest and Anna. They had just suffered the loss of their week-old baby and were distraught to the extent that it seemed that nobody could give them any consolation whatsoever. Padre spent an hour with them, and succeeded where we all had failed. He gave them solace and understanding and a measure of peace.

9

RETURN TO NEW ZEALAND

On December 30, 1970, a few months after Susanne's return to New Zealand, our second daughter was born in a maternity home in Wellington. I was still in Europe, working in a bank at a job I had begun to loathe. Upon my arrival in New Zeeland, I was greeted by a pleasant surprise – Susanne had bought, with her father's help, a modest but lovely little house in a pleasant suburb of Wellington. Of course, that meant mortgage payments, etc., so I began looking for work almost immediately. I found work as a waiter/barman in a Wellington bar, but I soon began to realize that all I wanted to do was continue studying and become a teacher.

In early 1971 I was accepted as an untrained secondary school teacher in a large school fifteen miles from Wellington and that would mark the beginning of my life in education. Being a secondary school teacher in New Zealand in the seventies had its advantages, as well as its disadvantages. On the positive side, the job offered plenty of opportunities to interact and work with students, parents, and other teachers. It also offered the opportunity to understand the purpose of education and its methods, while leaving one with a lot of free time to pursue other interests. However, the trade-off was a continual struggle to make ends meets, as salaries then were appallingly low.

By 1973, my relationship with Susanne had reached breaking point and we were soon separated. A year later we were divorced. I was distraught at the thought of not being a part of my daughters' lives, and over the years I have wondered if they suffered much as a result of my absence, especially after my departure from New Zealand two years after the divorce.

In order to forget the pain and the growing guilt the divorce had brought about, I joined in the efforts to set up a seaside commune an hour north of Wellington, and it was there that I spent some of the happiest and most meaningful moments of my life. The commune comprised ten people of various backgrounds and they became my new family. Sally, a language teacher who worked in the same school, became my companion. She was from the South Island and had an enormous capacity for life. She shared my hut, which was equipped with a sandpit for a toilet. The Paekakariki Commune – as it was known – was largely self-reliant, and we cultivated our own vegetables, recycled as much as we could, and made money renovating old furniture. The solidarity and friendship that I experienced over shared meals and tasks, the proximity to nature, and the non-individualistic and non-materialistic way of life led to a very fulfilling experience. Later, along with Linda – an American teacher – I bought a small farm nearby and planted hundreds of trees on it. And then, with the aspiration of immersing myself completely in nature, I began to work on a blueberry plantation; but the land was meant for grazing and would not cooperate in bringing to fruition my ill-conceived plans.

Life in the commune was easy and blissful. However, it was also too self-centred and completely closed. I was always conscious of the fact that outside, in the wider and less privileged world, there were large problems to be solved and it seemed increasingly like an act of selfishness to continue living there. Soon after I received my MA I decided to leave for Europe, even though that would mean seeing my daughters even less than the weekends when I would visit them.

In choosing to return to Europe I was essentially handing over all responsibility for my daughters' upbringing to Susanne, and it is only recently that I have become fully aware of the struggles and pains that she had to go through as a single mother and how these have impacted Olga and Michele. Their lives were further complicated by Susanne's second marriage to an alcoholic man, the birth of another daughter, another divorce, and the fact that she did not receive any support from her family while going through this ordeal.

There is no doubt that Olga and Michele suffered much as a result of my departure and absence, and I have often wondered if they considered that I'd abandoned them. It has undoubtedly contributed to their emotional fragility – especially Olga, who seems to feel insufficiently loved and appreciated by her father. This situation has pained me throughout my life and it is only now, with the help of an Australian counsellor, and through regular contacts with Olga, that we've finally begun to bridge what had long seemed an impossible divide.

10

RETURN TO EUROPE

I returned to Europe in the winter of 1976, full of uncertainty and questions that I just did not have the answers to. Accustomed to the easygoing life in New Zealand, Europe in its winter gloom and with its unremitting focus on the professional life seemed completely inhospitable to me. I found an excellent job in a government funded educational research institute in Geneva and started to work on issues similar to the ones I'd been working on in New Zealand – school related pressures, irrelevant syllabuses, cultural differences, the rights of ethnic minorities and absence of genuine inter-cultural dialogue, the labelling and neglect of socially handicapped children, the narrow-mindedness of teachers, and the hierarchical pettiness and sense of self-importance of bureaucrats.

My two years in the office proved to be both socially constructive and professionally disastrous. I had to leave the agency in a hurry after incurring the wrath of its rather pompous director, who refused to publish research outcomes that did not support his narrow world view.

I was outraged by the fact that the educational bureaucracy at the time fought tooth and nail to preserve its own privileges and perks and its twisted and narrow minded vision of education. The system itself, and some of its managers and teachers, were then, and perhaps still are, largely responsible for the fact that many children do not actually have access to a meaningful and relevant education, one that values and promotes their inner talents and potentials and satisfies their longing to learn. Children from lower socio-economic backgrounds, including foreign children – a large majority in most classes in Geneva – suffer most from this deplorable system-centred situation. Equally shocking is the fact, as I recently discovered, that over thirty years later the situation has not changed significantly: the issues remain the same and the feeble solutions proposed still fail to address the real causes of the problems; and the system itself still seems to be largely incapable of supporting and promoting the growth of the children's individual talent and potential. It is quite shocking to witness, across the planet – even in the highly developed West, the dismal failure of educational systems that emphasize competition over cooperation, individualism over solidarity, and academic achievements over the flowering of human goodness.

A call from the Federal Ministry of Foreign Affairs spared me the added embarrassment of having to appear in front of Geneva Republic's administrative tribunal questioning the right of a researcher to publish the outcomes of investigations that were detrimental to the administration itself but helpful to pupils and their parents. They were offering me an interesting if somewhat tricky two-year long position in Chad, where I was to work at strengthening the capacities of colleges serving the needs of young farmers.

However, while my professional troubles were fomenting, my personal life was blooming. It was while working there that I met Judy, a sort of soul sister, and it was she who suggested that I ought to go and listen to an exceptional Indian spiritual teacher – Krishnamurti. For me, the encounter with Krishnamurti – a frail, old, and totally unassuming little man – was a life transforming experience. His message was terse, clear, and completely revolutionary, while being profoundly practical at the same time, and it has been a source of guidance and inspiration to me up to this day.

More importantly, working at the office meant that I also met Claire, an intelligent and dedicated humanitarian and professor from

Haiti. I am unlikely to ever forget the way we met on the Geneva University stairs on a bright and warm August morning in 1978. I was in charge of registering the names of the two hundred delegates who had been invited to a week long educational congress by my agency, and when I first saw the glorious creature walk up the stairs towards me, I almost fell apart.

We would be married a few months later in a small Quebec town, and I, for the first time in my life, would know an all-consuming love and passion, and would learn the pain of attachment and dependence on another being.

A new family, then, with Claire and her two children; a new life, first in Switzerland, and then in West Africa. But it would not last long.

Three years after we were married, I received a call from Susanne's family regarding Olga and Michele, and how they were on the verge of becoming delinquents. Claire refused to travel with me to New Zealand, and I had come to the conclusion that my first and foremost duty was to my daughters rather than my second wife. I abandoned her and the job and returned to New Zealand, only for Susanne to tell me that the situation was now under control and that instead of taking over the upbringing of the girls – as was originally planned – I would be allowed to see them only once every six weeks. Meanwhile, Claire had returned to Canada, where the divorce had been pronounced. Utterly frustrated, I returned to Europe to complete my doctorate at London University.

Part II

Out Into the World

11

AFRICA

Despite the threat of imminent war in Chad – one of the most economically depressed and politically unstable countries at the time – my Belgian colleague, Robert, a rural sociologist, and I left Europe for Africa in early 1979 and commenced work at once with a great deal of enthusiasm. The job involved, as a first step, an overall evaluation of the functioning and impact of a series of rural colleges meant to inform, educate, and train destitute, unskilled, and mostly illiterate young farmers from across the country. The second part of the assignment involved the implementation of a series of measures aimed at strengthening such vital institutions, while the ultimate objective was to contribute to the reduction of serious and widespread rural poverty. Two years had been set aside to accomplish this rather ambitious task and two social scientists (Robert and I) had been recruited to carry it out. This was my first experience of the field, and I ventured forth with a great deal of excitement.

Some six weeks after our arrival in N'Djamena, the capital, a ferocious civil war between rival northern and southern factions suddenly broke out. The French army in Chad had received orders to evacuate all French expatriates – numbering in the hundreds – and also all Swiss foreign aid workers from the country. We were twelve in all, scattered across the country, and were to be picked up from our homes and evacuated to neighbouring Cameroon. In the confusion and turmoil, the French army at first completely forgot us Swiss aid workers and for a while we were left behind in our own villas, unable to get out, and completely terrified.

Early one morning I was woken up by a powerful and insistent knock on the door of my villa. A smart young French army officer standing outside saluted and informed me that I had exactly five minutes to pack up and leave for the airport. At the airport, a large French army transport plane was waiting, engine running. Inside were a whole lot of distressed white faces, anxiously waiting to take off and escape the shells. To my surprise and relief, I found my colleague, Robert in the plane. He was exhausted – he had spent the last few days hiding under the kitchen sink of his villa at the centre of N'Djamena so as to avoid being hit by stray bullets. The first thing he said to me was, "Hell, I'm glad to see you again, man."

Some of the passengers were wounded, and we were told that the French Government had managed to convince the two Chadian factions fighting each other for power and control of the country to hold an hour-long cease fire so as to allow the evacuation of expatriates. After some hours, the plane landed in Yaoundé, the capital of neighbouring Cameroon, where I spent a week nursing a cold, recuperating, and wondering about the future of my work in Chad.

Thus ended my first array into the so-called Third World. A mission that was meant to last two years had been terminated in two months, its goals unfulfilled and the donors' money wasted. The experience left me shaken. It was hard to accept the fact that a few power hungry men could so easily destroy years of hard work and leave an entire population so destitute and terrified, their hopes and aspirations all shattered.

However, in the few weeks there I had also begun to understand that given a degree of support and absence of external interference these people – some of the poorest in the world – were only too able to lift themselves out of the mire of degrading poverty and deprivation, become self-reliant again, and regain their dignity and control over their own destiny. And thirty years spent in over thirty of the poorest countries on Earth has solidified this understanding into an incontestable belief.

There were personal lessons too. Late one afternoon in February 1979 in a remote region of the country, a sous-préfet (head of a district administration) requested to see me and my team before our return to the capital. The charming gentleman asked me if he, as an African, could make a suggestion. I, always keen to learn about Africa, acquiesced. In a soft voice the sous-préfet said: "I understand that this is your first time in Africa. I have observed you during your mission in this remote region of our poor country. I understand that you are Swiss and I have seen that you are a dedicated, serious, and hard working young man. I have also understood that you are devoted to your work and are deeply respectful of Africa and Africans. Therefore, I am making the following suggestion. If you want to succeed in your work in Africa at any level and in any circle, you will always have to, first and foremost, take time to establish genuine and meaningful human rapport. If you do that, you will see that your work as a Western adviser in Africa will not only be greatly facilitated but most probably successful." I have remembered this almost daily over the last twenty-eight years, and it has proved extremely useful in every country in Africa and in other continents as well.

Unfortunately, Chad, thirty years later, remains as poor and ill governed as ever. As is the case in all too many developing countries, political instability, human greed, corruption and incompetence – especially at the highest levels of society – are largely responsible for this state of affairs. Self-centred politicians pursue their destructive power games, their meddling, and their lies; bureaucrats continue to steal from, and abuse, their own people; and Western donors keep on proposing schemes, programmes, and strategies that are neat on paper but do nothing to address ground realities, while at the same time supporting the national elites by turning a blind eye to their corruption and their incompetence; and all this in the name of "Saving Africa", or some such catchy slogan.

Also, the true role of France – the former colonial power – in this continuing turmoil has unfortunately never been analysed or fully disclosed, but the root of the conflict can be traced to the creation, by France, of artificial and arbitrary boundaries across different ethnic groups. And this, along with the plundering of natural resources and the failure to train and educate the general population, is true not only of Chad but of every former colony across the continent.

The exile from Chad was to last, according to the predictions of experienced diplomats, only a few days; however, this prediction never materialized, as the war was to spread havoc and destruction all across the country. Instead of returning all Swiss foreign aid workers were ordered back to the safety of Bern and the tedium of bureaucratic life. Here, I met Hans Peter, who had also recently been evacuated from Central America. A survivor and a pioneer in several ways, he and I would become life-long friends, and to this day we visit each other to reminisce about the past and complain about the present state of the world.

It would be two years before I finally returned to Africa; this time to Burkina Faso, as an adviser to the Ministry of Female and Social Affairs. My new home for the next three years was to be hot, dry, and dusty Ouagadougou – the capital, then known as the world's largest village.

Burkina Faso was still known as Upper Volta at the time, and my task there was to investigate some of the major problems affecting neglected minorities, especially women and children; make recommendations; and implement the same with a team of national counterparts. My boss, the minister, was a woman who, unfortunately, had adopted all of her male colleagues' devious practices, including corruption. She took quite a dislike towards me – especially as I knew far too much about her corrupt practices and her incompetence – and tried, unsuccessfully, to sack me. However, a few months later, she herself ended up in front of the popular street courts after being caught attempting to flee with the ministry's silverware.

I, of course, would stay for another two years, learning to appreciate the extraordinary kindness and humanity of the country's people. And it was this kindness and warmth while facing the privations of extreme economic hardship that convinced me to explore the country and the people further, as I believed that they had valuable lessons to teach Westerners sufficiently humble and open to the experience. And it was this exploration that would provide the base materials for my PhD thesis, which was titled "Popular Participation in Basic Education in the African Sahel".

Among the most acute problems facing the country then, and possibly even today, were poor governance by incompetent military regimes; grave shortages of water, food, and electricity; poor transport and communication; frequent drought; widespread illiteracy and lack of access to education; serious gender discrimination; a catastrophic health care situation; and widespread unemployment and youth delinquency. It was assumed at the time by both the national government and donors that the setting up of community-based and women-managed multi-function centres all over the large and under-populated country would contribute to solve some of these issues. The decision to set up the centres, however, had been taken without the participation of the supposed future beneficiaries themselves – the village women, and this would lead to many difficulties later.

Over a three years period, I – in my capacity as the foreign "expert" – would assume responsibility for setting up the centres in specific locations while guiding and providing support for a team of national civil servants. The participation of local populations though active was partially forced, and we provided basic literacy and training in simple income generating skills so as to encourage the illiterate female participants to become more self-reliant and gain a degree of freedom from the domination and abuse of their men. Unfortunately, the selection of skills to teach were determined by detached and ill-informed bureaucrats rather than being based on local demand and dialogue with the concerned population. This approach I would see replicated again in Bangladesh and several other countries, and the lessons learnt from the failures in one country never seem to be passed on to another. This top-down, non-participatory approach to decision making, and the imposition from outside, have been the cause of many a failed development programme.

Unsurprisingly, numerous obstacles emerged as soon as we began. Many of the problems were as a result of the meddling of politicians and bureaucrats (all men). However, insufficient and lackadaisical pre-programme preparation and planning and the irrelevance of the programme contents were key factors as well. Added to that was the greed, self-centredness, and jealousy of the village men. The female beneficiaries would be constantly intimidated by their husbands and other men, many of whom behaved as if the potential economic success of the women and their subsequent autonomy were a threat to them and their egos. And investigations showed that many men were indeed very worried about the women's success and the self-assertion that might well follow.

Female genital mutilation at the tender age of nine was a common practice even though it was illegal, and it took me almost a year to understand the origin of this barbaric and dangerous rite. Women colleagues were initially reluctant to talk about the practice, and it was only after I had earned their trust that they were willing to share their thoughts on the matter with me. They were quite unequivocal in their condemnation of the practice, and in their view that it had been imposed long ago by men as a means of subjugating women. It was then believed that if women took too much pleasure in sexual activities, they may be tempted into having more than one lover and this may lead them to lose sexual interest in their own husbands; as a consequence, the sexual appetite and enjoyment of women had to be curtailed and, thus, the clitoris removed in a dangerous, and often fatal, operation carried out by unskilled and ignorant old women.

As is the case in many poor countries, young and mostly uneducated women were forced to turn to prostitution in order to feed themselves and contribute to the family income. This situation had become quite problematic in Burkina Faso in the eighties and it has probably grown worse over the years. Such prostitutes were often modern day slaves at the mercy of cruel and perverse pimps. In the early eighties a few professional women, mostly teachers, in the Northern city of Ouahigouya got together and decided to do something concrete and lasting for their much less fortunate soeurs de la brousse (sisters from the savannah). The leader of the teachers, Madeleine Barry – a brave and jolly matron – was the engine behind the action. She, along with her colleagues created an association named l'Association des Femmes Burkinabes de Ouahigouya. The association grew rapidly, and with the participation of the illiterate women from a growing number of surrounding villages, it set up small but sound income generating programmes which largely contributed to positively transform the life of many women.

With the help of some Swiss NGOs, I was able to contribute to some of the programmes by setting up La Maison de la Femme in Ouahigouya itself. Here village women could learn new skills, exchange views and experiences with other women, and even seek shelter from abusive husbands. The success of this initiative was without a doubt due to the fact that is was locally conceived and run by competent and dedicated women responding to the needs and aspirations of village women.

As had been the case before, the attitudes and behaviour of men quickly became an obstacle to the success of Ouahigouya women. Confronted with the economic successes of an increasing number of village women, many men reacted with chauvinistic envy and spite. Some of the men – including husbands of the teachers involved – destroyed irrigation systems that the women had built to water their vegetable gardens.

The unchecked dominance of men; their lack of respect towards women; and the absence of support for, and the appreciation of, women's strengths and uniqueness often came as a shock, and contributed much to the lack of progress in village communities. In a few villages – Kougsabla being one of them – men finally understood progress was impossible without the active and equal involvement of women in the affairs of the village. One evening, Kougsabla's Council of Elders – composed entirely of men – issued the following declaration following a meeting with me under the palaver tree: "We have come to understand that some of our own traditions often represent serious obstacles in our attempts to improve our village's living conditions. Discrimination and oppression of women is an example of a bad tradition that needs to be discarded if we are to progress as a community. We have now also clearly understood that men must actively support the women rather than try to control them and erect obstacles in whatever they are doing. We do very much need women, and we need to change some of our old ways and habits. We need to complement what the women are doing rather than fight it." Never before had I heard something so liberating come from the mouth of an illiterate old man, and it was a deeply moving experience.

As an idealistic European working in West Africa, in an institution meant to contribute to alleviate people's suffering, I had been given a unique opportunity to witness first hand the African way of functioning and coping with life's uncertainties. This allowed me to observe the vast differences in priorities and functioning between women and men. Women were on the whole more concerned about the welfare of others, especially of children. In most cases, women were better listeners and they were also better at pursuing solutions to the end, regardless of obstacles. They were also more tolerant and patient and hardly ever passed judgement or blamed others, unlike many of the men.

From illiterate village women I learned about the extraordinary courage and resilience of the human spirit, and I began slowly to understand the immense price to be paid by countries that treat half of their population as second class citizens and do not give them a fair chance of fulfilling their own potential. Such countries, alas, still exist, and they will probably never be able to fully escape poverty, political instability, and socio-economic stagnation.

12

REVOLUTION AND FRIENDSHIP

Over the course of the three years I spent in Burkina Faso, I was witness to six military coups d'état, with each coup heralding the arrival of a new incompetent – usually a pompous military man pretending to defend the people's rights.

The emergence, then, in the middle of such chaos, of a young, intelligent, and dedicated captain, Thomas Sankara, was like a breath of fresh air. Thomas Sankara had a sound vision for Africa. He quite correctly felt that Africans, if they were to get rid of abject poverty, once and for all, had to rely on themselves and on themselves alone. Foreign assistance, especially the "assistance" from the former colonial master, France, had to be limited, as well as seriously scrutinized. This courageous and positive vision on the part of an unknown Burkinabe captain irritated many people, including the French political elite and its African allies, who were nothing more than puppets. Thomas Sankara was murdered, and with his death died his vision for Africa. His assassination was probably planned by French authorities and it was executed by one of his best friends, another Burkinabe captain, who, in turn, was pushed out of power by rebellious youths a few months ago after twenty-seven years of power abuse and failure to contribute to the development of his country.

One evening, I was driving when I heard loud horns behind me. I looked in the mirror and saw lights flashing and immediately thought I was being pursued by bandits. I accelerated, but not for long; an old man who'd been riding a bicycle was now on the hood of my car. Thankfully, he was uninjured. Four men got off the car pursuing me and walked towards me. One of them – a tall and elegant gentleman – introduced himself as the chief of Ougadougou police. I tried to explain why I was driving so fast, but he was adamant that I had to spend a night in prison. I did, and it did serve its purpose – from then on I took greater care driving.

That night in the courtyard of Ouagadougou prison was one of the most memorable experiences I've ever had. I had feared a night of brutality and humiliations; instead, I was treated with kindness and concern. There were over three hundred prisoners – including one woman – and some of them had been there for years, some for petty offence, others without even knowing the reason why. Having apologized to the police chief for my behaviour, I left the prison early next morning in the company of the representative of the Swiss consulate. It was almost painful to part from my new found friends, especially knowing that most of them would continue to languish there for months, even years.

Meanwhile, I was adopted by the village of Kougsabla (literally, black stone). It was my reward for the efforts I'd made in providing practical and financial assistance to the village through some Swiss NGOs. The adoption ceremony took place in the middle of the night, in pitch darkness. It was conducted entirely by the village women, who performed strange rituals and chanted before declaring that I – who was dressed rather ridiculously in all white African pyjamas – was now, and would be until the end of time, a son of the village.

This kindness and spontaneity was evident across all levels of society in Burkina Faso, and it meant even work would often take a back seat for a ritual expression of friendship, etc. I still remember quite vividly spending three hours in the sun and dust being introduced to, and greeting, each and every villager in Kougsabla – over three hundred of them. By the time the work started, I was thoroughly exhausted; nonetheless, we continued to work well into the night, under the light of the moon, stung regularly by the mosquitoes. That night I slept outside – it being too hot to sleep in the hut; I was given a two centimetre thick mattress and a young woman was tasked with watching over me and chasing away the mosquitoes.

One day, in the middle of the busy and dusty main street of Ouagadougou, I was overcome by uncontrollable emotion and burst into tears. They were tears both of joy and sadness: I had suddenly recalled the many acts of kindness and warmth in this destitute, poverty-stricken country; I was struck by the realization that there could still be in this cruel world places where such selflessness and goodness could flourish. Years later, in Senegal, something similar would happen with my daughters.

I had made friends in Ouagadougou too, and these consisted of three Burkinabe bureaucrats, a French artist, and an Italian farmer from Aosta who had married a local girl. We met every week around warm beer and king size French fries and in so doing created lasting ties of friendship and trust. By the time I left Burkina Faso at the end of my tenure, I had in many ways become African – I had learnt well, and have never since forgotten, its lessons in humanity and the sanctity of friendship.

13

JOURNEY ACROSS AFRICA

Mali

In 1985, a Switzerland based Catholic aid organization, Caritas, invited me to carry out an intensive eight week long mission in Mali. The purpose of the mission was to assess development work carried out over many years by the White Fathers – a religious order – in several remote regions of that vast country. Mali – a vast, largely sand covered Sahelian country four times the size of France, south of the Sahara – was in the eighties a magical and unique country. There was much to see and experience there, including Timbuktu, a spectacular but remote desert city; Bandiagara, with its cliffs and its troglodytes practising a lifestyle that has changed little over the centuries; Salif Keita and his incredibly nostalgic and evocative music; the seemingly endless sun-scorched land where in the evenings the sun plunged from the sky and disappeared abruptly behind the distant sand dunes.

Because of the size of the country, the remoteness of many of its regional centres, inadequate transport and communication infrastructures, and extreme climatic conditions, the mission quickly became a frantic race against time. Accompanied by a Malian translator and a very competent driver, I had to cover, over the course of the eight weeks, thousands of miles on dusty and barely visible dirt roads, all the while meeting and interviewing scores of people, from missionaries to local administrators. In the end, it turned out to be quite an ordeal.

The White Fathers were all Europeans; single; and highly skilled in specific trades, such as carpentry, mechanics, electricity, plumbing, etc. Having lived in the country for decades, they were fluent in local languages, and they made a deep and lasting impression on me. Their dedication, commitment, and courage; their closeness to, and respect for, rural populations; their pragmatism; their selflessness and sense of humour; all of these became to me essential lessons in humanity and what real partnerships in development efforts should be like.

Prior to arriving in Mali, I had imagined a mission full of obstacles, with bigoted and narrow minded missionaries; insecure religious hierarchies questioning the purpose and value of external evaluations; uncooperative bureaucrats and local politicians meddling with the mission's work; and local populations being stubborn and unresponsive towards my questions. However, not one of these imagined problems ever emerged; on the contrary, cooperation at all levels was total and prejudices completely absent, and White Fathers and White Sisters, along with regional politicians and administrators, greatly facilitated my work, while community members readily took part and offered many valuable insights related to their struggles.

Perhaps the most stirring and satisfying experience over the eight weeks of this mission was observing the extraordinary quality and depth of the relationships between the White Fathers and local communities. For the first time ever, I was witness to a situation where Africans and white Europeans were completely united in a joyful and caring partnership against poverty and neglect. All this made my return to the West, with all its preoccupations, more difficult. I longed to return to Mali, and for days on end I could not sleep or eat or function normally, aware that I had briefly experienced a new world and a way of life where humans could interact with one another on the basis of genuine care rather than selfishness and petty calculations.

And the White Fathers were not the only ones who made an impression upon me. The evening after my arrival I had visited a nearby bar. It was empty save for the barmaid. She was Awa Sangare, a gifted actress who had starred in Suleiman Cissé's "Finje" (The Wind) about a young Malian woman forced into prostitution in order to feed her children. She followed me, at least in my own imagination, throughout the mission and well beyond it.

And in Bandiagara, I met an old gentleman who had been a prisoner of war in Germany and spoke fluent German along with his impeccable French. His son, he proudly announced, was a member of the French football team. He fascinated me, and seemed to be the epitome of the African poet's description of wise old men who, when they die, are like libraries going up in flames.

At the end of the mission I had to go to Lomé, the sea side capital of Togo, to be debriefed by the Caritas representative for West Africa. He happened to be a priest and a quite brilliant sociologist. I met him in Lomé's imposing cathedral, where he asked a series of searching questions about the mission, its outcome, and the steps I would propose in order to pursue and strengthen the programme further. I immediately perceived that I was being interviewed not only by an exceptionally sharp mind but one that also displayed deep understanding and concern for his countrymen and their plight, and whose concerns were not limited to words alone but defined by actions and deeds in the field.

Niger

In Niger, another huge, desert-covered country in the Islamic Sahel, I and a colleague from the University of Geneva had to assess, on behalf of the Swiss Foreign Aid division, the impact of a literacy programme directed at destitute rural women. The mission ended in dismal failure. After two weeks of making every effort to gather and meet groups of village women beneficiaries so as to investigate their participation in the programme, we were forced to give up. The men in the villages were uncooperative and would not allow us to meet the women; they always had an excuse ready – either the women were busy in the fields or in the kitchen or with some ceremony or other. It was quite obvious that they did not want their women to have anything to do with us. In hindsight, the agency would have been better served sending two women, rather than two men, as evaluators; it was a deeply Islamic country, after all.

Gambia

Gambia is an English speaking former British colony in West Africa that stretches along the mighty Gambia river and is surrounded completely by French speaking Senegal. These political boundaries were arrived at by British and French colonialists to the obvious detriment of the local populations. My first contact with the country had been through the person of my friend, Fafa. However, the country itself displayed none of his flamboyance; instead it was a destitute playground for British and Swedish tourists.

The far Eastern, and very remote villages, of Gambia are inhabited by the Sarahoulé, a fiercely independent and proud tribe; and my mission was to investigate the reasons why the members of this tribe had, over the years, refused to send their children, especially their daughters, to modern schools. I was also required to propose solutions.

After long and patient questioning, the tribal leaders finally admitted that they were strongly opposed to the modern government schools. School makes girls bad, they said, and takes away from us our only wealth – our children. They, however, had no objection to sending their offspring to what they considered Koranic schools, even though they hardly provided any education at all.

My recommendation to the minister of education was to combine within one school elements from both modern and Koranic schools. But the recommendation was flatly rejected by the minister. He was furious and thought that such a move would result in large numbers of teachers and ministry officials losing their jobs. Once again, the interests and prerogatives of a system and institution had been considered to be more important than the needs and aspirations of local communities.

Senegal

Senegal has always been one of the pearls of the French colonial empire, with its oceans rich with fish; its mild climate; its rich culture, especially poetry and music; superb food; and its free press and democracy. However, the country has often proven a tough place to work for those involved in the development and foreign aid sectors. As is the case in many – if not all – countries in need of foreign aid, corruption, the self-centredness of governing elites, blatant cronyism, bureaucratic incompetence, and absence of transparency and lack of accountability were all part of Senegalese life in the early nineties.

I had been given a clear, if rather bizarre, mandate by my bosses in Geneva – go there and clean up the place. This was especially unusual because all I wanted to do was work in non industrialized countries for their development rather than act as a policeman defending Western interests in far away places.

Efforts to fulfil the policing part of the mandate often led to some awkward situations. My predecessor was a Frenchman who suffered from bouts of alcoholism and depression, and I was required to correct some of his mistakes. This meant revising strategies and making cuts to the budget for a large programme aimed at supporting village women organized into groups all over Senegal. The people affected by the budget cuts were obviously not happy and used all sorts of approaches in order to force me to retreat, including death threats, which were delivered at night by army officers. All through the ordeal I received little support from my bosses in Geneva. However, as the Dutch government was financially supporting the programme, the Dutch Embassy in Dakar were enormously supportive. And while I did not cave in to the demands, I did become quite sick as a result of all the pressure.

The idea of supporting rural women in various ways – offering functional literacy classes, labour market related skill training, small loans, etc. – was excellent; however, the interference of local officials and of men fearful of the women's success complicated things much to the detriment of a well-designed programme that could have been a model to emulate across other parts of Africa.

My year long Senegalese experience once again alerted me to the serious limitations of foreign aid, especially aid programmes implemented through multi-lateral agencies. Multi-lateral agencies, and to some extent large bilateral ones, tend to lack the knowledge and understanding of local communities, their real needs, and their aspirations and capacities, to be of any use as committed and equal long-term partners. And all too often, financial and administrative considerations and matters of prestige take precedence over the more essential human, psychological, and cultural considerations.

Tanzania

In April 1994, Rwanda a small East African country descended into anarchy as a result of a government led genocide that pitted the two main ethnic groups of the country – Hutus (the short ones) and the Tutsis (the long ones) – against each other. As a result, 800,000 people were killed – mostly by government supported militias – while millions others fled to neighbouring countries. Over a period of forty-eight hours over a million people with their cattle and their meagre belongings crossed into the Kagera province in Northern Tanzania, on the border with Uganda. The province, already destitute and neglected, was ill-prepared for such an influx, and the United Nations were given a mandate to lead and coordinate the international effort aimed at aiding the region.

I was asked to advise a team of national officials and foreign experts who were given forty-two million dollars by the international community to rehabilitate and reconstruct bridges, schools, roads, private houses, and agricultural fields. Conflict resolution was also part of the team's overall mandate, all of which had to be accomplished over an eighteen month period.

Once again lethargic bureaucracies, corruption, and government incompetence greatly impeded the implementation of the proposed rehabilitation programme. Most government officers saw the programme and the available funds as an opportunity to enrich themselves and increase their own individual prestige. Moreover, unduly strict schedules and time limits imposed by external donors proved to be grossly detrimental to the programme, largely based on regional extension workers and village based volunteers, all hastily trained and supported. Also, it was not a particularly easy experience working from a bunker type of compound with Rwandese Intarahme militias hiding in the nearby jungles and regularly attacking convoys of government officers and U.N. officials.

The sinking on Lake Victoria in May 1995 of the Bukoba, a ship loaded with over a thousand people, of which only forty-two survived, and the near riots that followed, only served to add to the difficulties. The situation was further exacerbated by the behaviour of some foreign-aid workers in charge of refugee camps – the expensive equipment, high salaries, flashy clothes, and cocky behaviour did little to placate the locals already trying to cope with the disruptions caused by the influx of refugees. In one district, prices of local commodities shot up sharply as soon as foreign workers arrived; this resulted in another exodus of people, this time fleeing high prices. In the end, as a result of poorly designed programmes and inadequate strategies, only a small part of the mission's overambitious objectives could be fulfilled.

Of course, Tanzania was not the Kagera region alone. There was the immense and protected Serengeti plains, with its amazing wild life and deep spirituality; the unique Olduwai gorge – the Cradle of Mankind; the magic wonder of the Ngorongoro Crater; and the stunning charm of some of Lake Victoria's shores. And exploring these did much to provide relief from the pressures and disillusionment of the work.

Burundi

Burundi – a small, landlocked country in East Africa – is populated, like Rwanda, by the Hutus and Tutsis, two ethnic groups that detest each other. I spent a few months there trying to understand the requirements of young people and analysing the government's capacity to respond to these. Burundi's potential is obvious, as it has all of the advantages of being small and inhabited by intelligent and hard working people, a pleasant climate, and decent infrastructure. Yet, the country seems incapable of breaking through and ending the vicious cycle of ethnic violence, government incompetence, and endemic corruption in which it has been caught for so long.

Ethiopia

Because of its position in East Africa, and its complicated history, Ethiopians seem to consider themselves different from most other Africans, with some even denying African identity. Over the years this vast and poverty stricken land has often been overrun by refugees from neighbouring countries, especially Sudan.

My stay here was brief but intense. My work focused on the educational needs of refugees and how they could be supported so that they could be self-reliant upon their return home. Apart from discovering the charm of Ethiopian food and music, and the thrill involved in flying in tiny planes that flew at the level of tree tops and landed on barely visible fields, I discovered there a rare jewel. It was an education and training programme dedicated to Sudanese refugees which promoted the self-reliance of these destitute and traumatized people.

In the course of a few years the programme – intelligently designed and run by an Irish NGO – became so successful that it drew in growing numbers of villagers from the recipient country and became a model of successful integration of refugees and locals and rural development; and it, along with its complementary facets – skill development, literacy, income generation, conflict resolution, economic self-reliance, etc. – would be emulated in the entire country and beyond.

The success was the outcome of at least three essential factors: intelligent and dedicated leadership; competent and transparent management; active local participation and involvement on the part of beneficiaries in the design, funding, implementation, monitoring and ownership of the programme; and absence of interference and control on the part of national and regional authorities and donors supporting the programme.

14

NEPAL

In September 1987, I was sent by the International Labour Organization (ILO) on a three year mission to Nepal to assume the role of Chief Technical Adviser in the field of vocational training to the government. My task was to lead a team composed of locally recruited personnel and ILO recruited international consultants in setting up three basic training centres for unskilled youth in the south of the poverty stricken Himalayan kingdom.

Nepal was to be as transformative an experience as Africa. Confronted again with the politicians and bureaucrats of a developing country, and foreign aid organizations with their frequently arrogant officials, I found my doubts about the efficacy of foreign aid growing. I also began to realize that little would change without a profound and very unlikely transformation in the mentality of the governing elites. I had observed at close quarters the nature of the relationship between assisted countries and the ones providing the assistance. Although people on both sides of the divide were constantly talking about things like "a partnership of equals", "local ownership", and other such fashionable but empty slogans, it was all too obvious that there was no equality at all between the two partners. And how could there be, when the donor country was the sole provider and made all the decisions while the recipient country requested, if not begged outright for, assistance? The relationship was obviously flawed from conception itself and was predicated on dependency, both financial and political. Nepal, in many ways, was a perfect illustration of the result of a skewed relationship between two countries.

Corruption at all levels of society is pervasive in most developing countries, and it is largely accepted as a standard and unavoidable practice. And one of the reasons for this is the easy availability, and access to, considerable amounts of money. As such, corruption is most virulent and obvious within government bureaucracies, especially at national level; and among politicians, with the involved parties often openly using aid money to further their own interests. Donor parties and multilateral aid agencies have contributed to the situation by either tacitly condoning, or worse, by actively contributing to the phenomenon by including a certain percentage of their budget to cover corruption related costs. And this acceptance of corruption as a fact of life rather than an ill to be fought against was perhaps the most depressing aspect of it all. To date, corruption remains one of the major contributory factors in project and programme failures worldwide and, also, in the persistence of poverty.

However, corruption was not the only ailment that Nepal was suffering from. An excessively self-centred and incompetent governing class that had proven itself quite incapable of providing a long term vision for the development of the nation; a poorly functioning, oversized, and ineffective bureaucracy; a largely inadequate education and training system, which led to a large proportion of the population being illiterate and unskilled; appalling communication, transport, and energy infrastructure all served – and unfortunately still do – to contribute to Nepal's lack of development.

Added to the above is its geographical position. Stuck between the two frequently quarrelling giants – China in the North and India in the South – Nepal has had to perform an exhausting balancing act, both in its foreign policy and its internal affairs, so as not to antagonize either one of them. Further complicating the situation is the regular interference of other world powers – for instance, the USA – especially in the elaboration of the country's development policies. Given such a scenario, it is not surprising that foreign aid schemes have all too often failed to reach the neediest and have contributed instead in reinforcing and strengthening corrupt institutions and practices.

In 1989, just over two years after my arrival in Nepal, the country was engulfed in a series of protests demanding democracy, better governance, and an end to corruption and neglect of the rural communities. The protests were initially peaceful; however, soon the army, on the King's order, began firing upon the protesters and killed a large number of people. A strict curfew was imposed, but despite that the country descended into anarchy and violence. During the disturbances, several courageous Kathmandu intellectuals – some friends of mine, and a number of foreigners joined the protesters to march upon the royal palace. Nepal – especially Kathmandu, its capital – was seeing, exactly two hundred years later, its version of the French Revolution.

In the end, the King consented to the demands of the protesters and absolute monarchy was abolished to be replaced by a constitutional monarchy. In the dirty and polluted streets of Kathmandu people celebrated their victory and a wave of euphoria and optimism swept through the country. A new constitution was written and a democratically elected government assumed power. Hopes were high, and the people believed that a fairer and more prosperous society would soon be theirs.

Alas, it took only six years for a much more serious problem to emerge in the form of a civil war between Maoists pretending to fight for the masses of poor people and the incompetent and corrupt government. Once again, hopes were quashed and Nepal descended into the chaos it had known for most of its history. And once again, the corruption, the incompetence, and the self-centredness of the governing classes were largely to blame. Since then, despite some feeble attempts at changing institutions and habits, the situation of Nepal has only worsened, so much so that during a recent visit I could only note with dismay and sadness that the country and its people were actually worse off than they had been twenty-four years earlier.

Despite the fact that Nepal has plenty of competent and selfless people, the absence of a competent and dedicated leadership and the lack of a long term and widely shared vision for the country continue to undermine any efforts to set the country on a path of sustained development. And this in spite of massive external assistance provided to the country. Sadly, it is hard to find any evidence of real progress in any major domain in Nepal today; instead, it seems that all the evidence points, rather, to regression. And although internal factors are predominantly responsible for Nepal's lack of development, foreign aid, with its often blind support of successive governments – no matter how weak – and its failure to foster desperately needed changes in policy and strategy has contributed its share. As a close Nepali friend has been pointing out for the last two decades, foreign aid has become more of a hindrance than a help. Aid in Nepal has not promoted the country's long term development; rather, it has stifled local initiatives and rendered the country largely dependent on external assistance.

The central problem with aid, according to some well informed and very concerned Nepali intellectuals, is the fact it has always been largely wasted. One of the main reasons for such wastage is that it is often given for the wrong reasons – to promote the immediate interests of donor countries rather than to assist and contribute to the long term development of Nepal and its suffering people.

And yet, despite so many repeated failures; shocking inequalities, largely sustained by the caste system; persistent and widespread poverty and injustice; and stifling pollution; large numbers of Westerners keep coming to Nepal. Undoubtedly, it is because of the stunning beauty and appeal of the Himalayas; the simplicity and friendliness of the Nepalese; and the exotic sense of mystery that still floats over this country, drawing in those that seek new frontiers and challenges, both physical and spiritual.

15

PAKISTAN

A three month stint in Karachi, Pakistan's sprawling commercial hub, although too short a time to appreciate all the nuances of the complex and tormented country's culture and people, does give one a fair idea about the complexity of a country that seems at times unable to decide whether it is a failed state or a country that is actually going somewhere. My main task was contributing to the strengthening of the National Institutc for Labour Administration Training (NILAT). Although short, the mission provided excellent opportunities to discover the potentials and weaknesses of the Pakistani training system and to fraternize with staff and students, and through them, discover some aspects of Pakistani society.

Despite the heat and anxiety of living in Karachi, I thoroughly enjoyed my stay there. I was put up at the Sindh Men's Club – a posh, old, colonial club, and there met, and exchanged views with, generals, politicians, and professionals. The conversations were intelligent and frank; perhaps because the place was one where people let both their hair and their guard down. Even the proudest and most nationalistic of generals admitted that the ongoing conflict between India and Pakistan was an absurdity that had to stop. After all, as a serving general stated,

Indians and Pakistanis were cousins and shared a common history, a common language, along with many cultural and artistic traditions.

However, on the streets of Karachi it was not rare to see gatherings of bearded, pyjama clad young men vehemently asserting the values and preponderance of Islam and Shariah law over all other religions and socio-political arrangements. Also, much to the anxiety of Westerners, Allah was frequently invoked while flying in Pakistan, where the pilots' customary announcements prior to take off and landing always ended with the announcement that everybody's fate was ultimately in his hands and that Inchallah (God Willing) the plane would take off or land as planned.

My friendship with the son of a former politician also gave me a glimpse of Pakistani society's relationship with alcohol, which was officially forbidden. For example, I would be served beer only after 9 PM and only in my hotel room; that too, after providing a copy of my passport and provided I had no local guest. And yet, at the weekly dinner parties in my friend's sumptuous villa, Bordeaux and Scotch flowed and was consumed equally by men and women.

Visiting Peshawar, in the province bordering Afghanistan, was another revelation. One of the issues facing the city – apart from the frequent acts of terrorism – was the vast numbers of Afghani refugees. The generosity of Pakistanis towards their Afghan brethren was boundless and deeply touching, especially considering their own poverty and struggle to survive. I visited a vast refugee camp along the border, and in so doing found something to appreciate first hand the nature of human relationships in this troubled part of the world.

The camp manager, a jolly but fierce two metre tall former commander against the Soviets, greeted me warmly and showed me around the camp and introduced me to a number of refugees, all young men, but crippled either physically or psychologically. Most of the men in the camp's rehabilitation centre had fought under him and his dedication, devotion, and kindness towards them was very moving. While leaving the centre I felt someone pulling at my belt. It was a handsome twenty year old Afghani soldier; he was on a wheelchair. The manager translated for him while he pleaded with me to take him back to Switzerland for an operation that would remove the bullet lodged in his spine; else, he would be bound to the wheelchair for life.

By the time I left Pakistan my view of the country had changed completely from the one I had prior to my arrival. Having had the privilege of interacting with a cross section of Pakistanis, my prejudices and fears all appeared to have been founded on ignorance and soon disappeared for good. Instead, I was left with a very positive impression of the country.

16

BANGLADESH

Between 1999 and 2002, I spent four long and often arduous years in a country that has at times been described as a basket case. I was working for the Swedish Foreign Aid Division and with the Bangladeshi Government as a team leader and adviser in non formal education. The work was challenging and there were constant frustrations and disappointments as well as times of great joy.

Bangladesh is a country defined by extremes: a short but violent history; a geography that leaves it prone to serious flooding; the highest population density in the world; religious extremism; severe poverty; frequent strikes and eruptions of violence; and a general sense of uncertainty about the country's future. Given such a background, the intensity and difficulty of carrying out development work there provided me the opportunity to understand both the limitations and the potentials of such work. It was almost the perfect ground to investigate development related issues and to test innovative approaches.

Over the last thirty years Bangladesh politics has been dominated by two power-hungry and incompetent women from two rival political families, who together have contributed to the progressive destruction of their country. Between 1999 and 2002, for four years in a row, Bangladesh was declared the most corrupt country in the world by

Transparency International, and the Ministry of Education – where I was working – was considered the most corrupt in the country. However, the stature of these two women is not reflective of the status of women in general in Bangladesh. As far as urban women are concerned, the world has been witness to the scandalous treatment of young women working as garment workers in Dhaka's dangerous factories, often working twelve hours a day, seven days a week, for a monthly salary of less than forty US dollars. Their rural counterparts fare little better, often working fifteen hours or more a day in a heroic and selfless manner. Added to that, they have to attend to the needs and demands of their often self-centred husbands, their many children, and sometimes the extended family as well. In times of crisis – floods and other natural disasters, for instance – the women of Bangladesh often show astonishing courage and resilience and perform incredible feats of bravery and resourcefulness that a Westerner cannot help but feel a deep admiration and lasting respect for.

The literacy programme I was working on was supported by seven major donor countries and multilateral agencies and a multitude of NGOs. It had a target population of thirty million people and an unheard of budget of close to a billion US dollars. The agency ultimately responsible for the implementation and monitoring of this oversized programme was the Department of Mass Education. The programme was doomed to fail right from the start, and it was finally wound down after ten years during which vast sums of money – which had been carelessly handed in by donors – disappeared into the private pockets of government officials and politicians. Of course, the illiterate masses for whom the programme had been designed enjoyed none of its benefits and there were no tangible or lasting results.

However, in contrast with the tedium and lack of productivity involved in working with the ministry and the bureaucracy, working with rural communities was especially fulfilling and productive. This is usually the case not only in Bangladesh but all over the world. Serious community based extension workers, as well as committed experts and consultants know this and cherish contacts and exchanges with local communities more than anything else. It not only gives real meaning to their work but also allows for a real possibility of sustainable progress. Moreover, local communities, contrary to many beliefs, have a lot to share with, and to teach, open minded outsiders.

Development work at community level in economically depressed societies is often a vital and trans-formative effort that can have an immediate and direct positive impact on families and individuals; provided, of course, that local people are given the ability to decide and be fully involved. In contrast, work at central or national level is carried out by individuals who are remote – both physically and psychologically – from the people they are supposed to serve. More often than not, they are bored and underpaid civil servants who have little understanding of, and interest in, the needs, problems, and aspirations of the communities. Therefore, their commitment to them and to their own work is at best superficial and lukewarm. Moreover, staff turnover among civil servants is extremely high, and often civil servants are suddenly transferred to other departments and asked to perform tasks for which they are totally unprepared and uninterested in.

In Bangladesh, as in Africa, this lack of an effective bridge between rural communities and central government bureaucrats and civil servants is by far one of the most serious obstacles in top down development efforts. Villagers in Bangladesh, as in Africa, are afraid and deeply suspicious of government officials, and their interaction is limited to the times when the tax man comes to collect taxes and when the policeman comes to arrest people. On the other hand, bureaucrats at national level often look down upon rural people as being primitive, unintelligent, and unable to think clearly, and initiate development activities on their own. Such attitudes obviously are grossly erroneous and create a climate of non communication and mutual suspicion, bordering on hatred at times, and enough to render impossible any possibility of working together.

Foreign aid in Bangladesh is a massive industry often producing quite counterproductive results. Examples of donor interference are many; a few years ago, the head of the World Bank called the Prime

Minister of Bangladesh suggesting that 120 million dollars were at her disposal as a further loan for non formal educational programmes in Bangladesh. This loan would have been in addition to the many millions of dollars borrowed and being spent quite uselessly in the sector. The fact that future generations of the country would be saddled with debts they could not possibly repay do not seem to have concerned either the head of the World Bank or the Prime Minister.

Sweden – a country that I have always admired – has been involved in Bangladesh for a long time as a major donor; however, that admiration would receive a serious blow when I was told in Stockholm, while being debriefed, that the Swedish government was well aware of the scale of corruption in Bangladesh and of the fact that a significant amount of its taxpayer's money was being stolen by bureaucrats and politicians in Bangladesh, but there was little they could do. If they were to try and punish Bangladesh by withdrawing funds, another aid agency would step in immediately to replace them. Needless to say I was quite shocked and disturbed by the attitude.

17

CAMBODIA

Few countries in the world have had as ghastly a history as Cambodia, and few has been traumatized as much by outsiders and its own people alike. France acted for many years as its arrogant, exploitative, and often brutal colonial master; while America, in an attempt to destroy the Ho Chi Minh trail, secretly bombed it during the Vietnam War; in addition, they rather stupidly put into place a puppet government that was largely responsible for the emergence of the Khmer Rouges, who murdered over a quarter of the country's population and emptied the country's cities in an absurd attempt to transform Cambodian society into an uneducated peasant utopia. Subsequently, the Vietnamese invaded and occupied the country; they got rid of the Khmer Rouges and installed a prime minister of their preference; the very same prime minister who is still in power today and has become a feared dictator. Meanwhile, the country remains as poor and as miserable as ever, thanks to his incompetence, corruption, and cruelty.

Today, Cambodia remains a deeply traumatized nation still searching for its identity and waiting for some justice to relieve the pain of the past. However, the ongoing International Tribunal – on which they had placed so much hope – has become an expensive farce enacted by fearful and corrupt local lawyers and powerless international judges and directed by the powerful prime minister. Here too, the UN and its expensive and awkward procedures and incompetence have betrayed an entire people; much as it did in the early nineties, when it was tasked with running the country in the immediate aftermath of the departure of the Vietnamese.

Most Cambodians who managed to escape the Khmer Rouges ended up in refugee camps in Thailand, which I visited several times as a member of a team of foreign experts. And it was during these visits that I was able to gather from the refugees details of life in Cambodia under the Khmer Rouges. An old gentleman told me how soldiers had come to his home, asked for his four sons, and over the next four days, murdered them one by one in front of him. Unfortunately, stories like his were the norm, and today there isn't a single family in Cambodia which hasn't been directly and deeply affected by the horrors of the last fifty years. Most Cambodians are still reluctant to relate their own sad and often disturbing accounts, but when they do the pictures that emerge are almost always of a barbarism that is almost incredible to comprehend.

Roshane, who at the age of five was separated from her parents and forced into a child labour camp, and who is now making films about Cambodia during the Khmer Rouges reign, tells of how she went to Battambang in the Northern part of the country to ask Khieu Sampan – the president of the country during the time – why he and the other leaders did what they did. His answer was that he did not know what was going on then as all the decisions were taken by Pol Pot. Luc, a close friend of mine, escaped the butchery as he was in Paris completing his studies. When he returned to Phnom Penh, shorty after the Vietnamese had ended the Khmer Rouges' reign, he found that each and every one of his ten member family had been murdered. Their crime: they had been "intellectuals" – teachers, office workers, etc. The Khmer Rouges executed ninety percent of the teaching force in Cambodia during their four year reign of terror. And today, thirty-five years later, Cambodia's Ministry of Education, with the assistance of foreign donors, is still trying to reconstitute it.

Because of the horrors of the past, there is a lot of goodwill towards Cambodia, and rich countries have been generous in their assistance, perhaps out of a guilty conscience, for they have all been participants in one way or the other in the destruction of this small but magnificent country.

18

THAILAND

Thailand is a country that provides many things to many people – cheap sex and tenderness for frustrated and ageing Europeans; cultural oddities, glorious beaches, and spirituality for tourists; all of it wrapped in a low-cost but pleasant and secure package. Over the last few decades the so-called Land of Smiles – an effective slogan to lure tourists – has progressed from being a refuge for lonely and frustrated men to a tropical paradise overrun by invading hordes of hedonistic tourists. Tourism in Thailand has been the cause of changing local values and mentalities, and not always for the better.

Many Thais, who thirty years ago were steeped in traditional values where religion and the monarchy dominated, have now embraced Western profit-oriented values without being aware of the dangers it brings about – disruption in families, loss of social cohesion, the weakening of national identity, and a decrease in willingness to engage in dialogue and resolve conflicts peacefully. Increasingly bloody street protests and battles are an example of growing anger, polarization, and alienation within Thai society today. As for the future, nobody can be entirely sure what will happen once the long-reigning monarch passes.

Thailand wears several different masks, and the tendency is to disguise the less appealing facets of Thai culture. Most Thais tend to be nationalistic and proud of their country while completely oblivious to the country's shortcomings and difficulties. Foreigners – tourists and expatriates alike – are not always trusted or even liked; in fact, they are usually tolerated because they are an economical necessity. To see and understand the less positive aspects of Thailand takes times, especially for foreigners, for much of it hid beneath the veil of smiles – often artificial – and attentive service; the blind subservience to authority and power, especially to the monarchy; greed and corruption among businessmen and the political elite; and a great deal of hypocrisy and denial. The following anecdote will serve to illustrate the above.

I have been colleague with, and a friend of, Dr. Kla – a US educated government officer – for over thirty years. Four years ago, Thailand was again in the news, but this time it wasn't another coup or street protests; rather, it was the inhumane treatment of the Rohingas, a Burmese Muslim minority fleeing their country after harassment from the military government. Upon their arrival in Thai waters, the Thai army immediately towed their rickety boats back to the high seas and set them adrift without food or water. Most of the refugees died. I was shocked and tried to share my sense of concern and rage with my Thai friend and his wife, but to my surprise, the couple flatly rejected all the accusations directed at the Thai military by the local and foreign media and tried, instead, to justify their behaviour.

And this was not the first instance of brutality on the part of the Thai military. Years ago, Thai soldiers had routinely brutalized and raped Cambodian refugees who had sought their protection and assistance. And the Muslim rebellion in the south of the country could probably have been quelled easily had the Thai army and police been less brutal in dealing with the protesters.

Following the recent dismissal of a democratically elected prime minister by the Supreme Court, and yet another army coup, Thai politics continues to be characterized by the growing anger and differences between rival political forces representing the rural masses and the Bangkok elites, and there is a real possibility of civil war in the country – the former land of smiles.

19

THE PHILIPPINES

Over the years I have visited the Philippines a dozen times and have developed a good understanding of this vibrant society and its incurably romantic people. My first visit was in the late seventies, at the end of which I wrote an article entitled "The Gogo Girls of Manila". It depicted the life of Innocencia, a young woman struggling to feed her family of twelve in Negroes – a remote, poverty stricken island in the Visayas region. In the seventies, Negroes was still largely divided into vast haciendas run by a handful of powerful and ruthless land owners whose workforce consisted of destitute sugar-cane workers who were for all intents and purposes modern day slaves. Lacking necessary work skills, Innocencia – a stunningly beautiful and naive twenty year old – had no choice but become a "gogo" dancer at Bubbles, a bar in Manila's red light district. Like most Filipinas, Innocencia was selfless and loyal and her devotion to her family was unconditional – she would have done, and did, almost anything to ensure the family's welfare and survival. This made her an easy prey for lusty old men, mostly Westerners. I managed to persuade her to leave the job she hated and enrol in a typing school. She was assiduous, but her monthly allowance proved too small to feed the family in Negroes, and she soon returned to the bar.

Poverty in the Philippines, with its population of over a hundred million people, is still widespread; as also are corruption; cronyism; poor governance; violence, especially in Mindanao; gender discrimination; and socio-economic inequality. A social class made up of inept politicians, greedy bureaucrats, and amoral businessmen selfishly pursue their affairs at the expense of the vast majority of Filipinos, and in doing so it seems that they are actually sowing the seeds of future upheavals in this volatile country. Lately, though, with the election of a serious and competent president, there are signs of the political and socio-economic situation improving.

Serious gender discrimination is another issue. Women over thirty-five are often considered too old for work and it is almost impossible for them to find decent jobs. Given such a situation, many Filipinas choose to go overseas to find work, mostly as domestic workers, caregivers and nurses – jobs that often leave them open to exploitation. Often, they have to leave behind their children and grandparents and send back large portions of their meagre salaries. Moreover, many men view women as no more than sex toys and a large number of women are defenceless victims of male violence; women are under protected by current laws and social practices, and wife bashing is accepted as a form of control.

The role that the all-powerful Catholic Church plays in the politics and governance of the country has also been a major factor in this subjugation of women. Not only does it ensure that contraception and divorce remain unavailable, it also instils a sense of fear and guilt in the minds of the many poor and uneducated through pressure tactics and indoctrination – for instance, failing to go to church on Sundays and not obeying the church's dictates are considered sinful acts for which retribution can be expected. The Catholic Church of the Philippines has largely failed as an institution meant to offer moral solace and spiritual guidance to a desperately poor and under-educated population; instead, it has succeeded in ensuring the continuation of oppression, ignorance, and poverty.

Today, most of the hopes and aspirations brought about by the 1986 People Power Revolution have largely disappeared to be replaced, instead, by growing cynicism and disillusionment, especially among the intelligentsia. Most Filipino social commentators today deplore the disappearance of the powerful collective spirit and drive that nourished an entire generation of young Filipinos in the eighties. Their lofty ideals seem to have vanished into the machinations of a socio-economic and political system that is slowly but surely driving the country toward the abyss that is a failed state. It is as though an entire nation has lost its compass and its will to fight. This situation has, of course, been exploited by corrupt and self-serving governing elites working closely with their allies – big businesses and the Catholic Church – in order to further their own interests. And today, more than ever, people in the country seem to seek solace and escape in mindless entertainment, celebrity worship, consumerism, the church, and the actual act of fleeing overseas.

In many ways, much of the country's difficulties – both past and present – are to an extent the outcome of its brutal colonial heritage. The Philippines were ruled for close to 300 years by the Spanish – historically one of the most ruthless and cruel colonizers, although their atrocities in the Philippines have not been detailed to the extent of the Conquistadors' in the Americas. A stroll in the pleasant Luneta Park in Manila can be a useful source of information regarding the horrors of Spanish rule and the courage of a handful of Filipinos who tried to resist them. The memory of Dr. Rizal – the heroic resistance fighter – who, along with his comrades, was executed by the Spanish authorities persist to this day and his deeds remain a source of pride and inspiration.

Spanish arrogance and excesses were replaced by milder forms of both when the Americans took over the country and transformed it into a vassal state meant to provide cheap labour, including soldiers; easy profits; and a convenient and defenceless scapegoat. And this persisted until the foreigners were finally driven away by both natural forces – the mighty eruption, in the nineties, of Pinatubo near two huge US military bases, and the relentless but peaceful protests for which the Philippines had been much admired all over the world.

One of the worst outcomes of colonization is the widespread destruction of self-esteem, dignity, and sense of identity of the entire nation. This is particularly true of the Philippines, where many Filipinos still seem to suffer from deep-rooted inferiority complexes, especially when interacting with foreigners. Low self-esteem, a tendency to underestimate one's own capacities while belittling one's talents and achievements, and ready acceptance of others' judgement and guidance are some of the characteristic traits of the Filipino mind. One example of this is Cory Aquino – the widow of the assassinated opposition leader and the mother of the current president. She went on to become president of the Philippines herself, and yet almost always described herself as a simple housewife.

There is no doubt that the future of the Philippines will depend largely on its women and on their capacity to overcome existing attitudes and social arrangements and impose their own views and qualities. This will be met with resistance by Filipino men, who will perceive women's attempts to liberate themselves as a serious threat to their own fragile egos. However, in the long run, the liberation of women will do as much for the men as the women themselves, as freer and economically independent women will contribute enormously to the country's progress.

The Philippines is blessed with immense potential; yet these are continuously stifled, not only by politicians but also by the people, with their widespread fatalism, lack of self confidence, and gross underestimation of their capacity to transform and rebuild their society. However, such a transformation would also require fundamental changes in the attitudes of men; but if successful could provide a solid foundation upon which to build a stronger and fairer society.

And the rest of the world, too, could benefit from adopting many aspects of the Filipino value system and some of its basic social units and arrangements, as reflected, for example, in the extended family; the closely knit rural community; and the relationships between friends, which display levels of solidarity and mutual concern rarely seen in the Western world. Rural Filipino society – which comprises the majority of the people – today still display levels of social harmony, mutual support, and solidarity rarely seen in more urban settings. It is as if geographic isolation and a lack of access to external public services have combined to bring about the best in the people and they have remained free of the debts that modernity demands of society – the loss of communal spirit and conviviality and solidarity.

The Philippines has much natural beauty and endless reserves of natural resources, along with the capacity and talent of its many ethnic groups and traditions. Known the world over for their artistic talents and their joie de vivre, Filipinos have been providing loving care to neglected patients, the elderly, and children in every corner of the world. They man ships, construction sites, and restaurant kitchens in numerous countries, and offer their contagious smiles to countless numbers of downtrodden in their lonely existence. Filipinos, in many ways, embody the fast-disappearing values of selflessness, solidarity, and loyalty; and, in doing so, they have become a source of light in a world growing increasingly dark.

One out of ten Filipinos (about ten million in total) lives and works abroad, and their contribution represents a large portion of the Filipino GNP. Yet, within the Philippines itself, the Filipino potential remains largely untapped, and the political class is clearly responsible for this. Even today, most leaders fail to appreciate and support the development of the many talents that Filipinos are born with and they still lack a comprehensive vision for the future of this magnificent country.

As is the case elsewhere, in the Philippines, too, education has long served as a means to mould children to fit into increasingly sick and dangerous societies, while serving also as a tool to manipulate rather than bring out a child's potential. In that respect, the education system has largely failed, and will continue to fail, the people of the Philippines; and instead of being an indispensable instrument in the uplifting of people, it appears to contribute to keeping a vast number of people in their current situation. Instead of opening the mind and encouraging critical thinking and serious questioning and analysis, the system appears to encourage rote learning and the accumulation of often useless information, all the while instilling the children an acceptance of existing socio-political arrangements and norms. The surprising lack of curiosity about, and knowledge of, the outside world; human rights; civic responsibilities and obligations; the environment; and an equal lack of interest in subjects such as philosophy can frustrate external observers. But these are outcomes of an inadequate and partly irrelevant national learning system that is defined by a lack of discipline; weak long term planning and organization; insufficient concern about and attention to the future and the consequences of certain actions.

If educational authorities in the Philippines were to be serious about the much discussed school reforms, then, perhaps, a real home-grown learning system – which, as experience has shown, has a better chance of succeeding – may emerge. However, for this to happen, communities must be given the resources, along with the power and the support, to decide and to develop their own systems and approaches; as is being successfully implemented through the School in a Box (or School without Walls) programme in South India by the Rishi Valley Educational Centre.

20

INDIA

It has been observed that a Westerner arriving for the first time on the Indian subcontinent is likely to have a few possible reactions immediately. Either they feel immediately terrified, bewildered, and threatened; or they are amazed and filled with a profound sense of curiosity. There is the physical discomfort to begin with – the stifling heat, overpowering smells, and deafening noises. There is also the feeling of one's senses and certainties being constantly assaulted and questioned, and the feeling that one's usual standards cannot be relied upon any more. The dominant feeling, however, is one of great confusion and of being lost in a sea of contradictory impressions and emotions. A life time spent in India would still not be enough to understand completely the complexity and depth of this vast nation, more a subcontinent than a country.

Truth seekers in India – and over the years there have been countless numbers of these dissatisfied Westerners – seem often to find some responses, even if only temporary, to their spiritual questions in India, whether it is through some guru, or the study of the Bhagavad Gita and the Upanishads, yoga, meditation, the repeating of mantras, etc. The fascination (or repulsion) that most visitors feel seems to be conditioned by their view of how religion and spirituality are approached and practised openly in India. Religion in all its forms and its numerous rituals and precepts is an integral part of everyday life in India over all strata of society. Vast amounts of time, energy, and money are expended upon apparently meaningless religious activities. Though often ruinous to poor families, this is the price to be paid for salvation upon death. The belief in reincarnation is widespread and strong; as is the appalling practice of categorizing people into castes.

The persistence of the caste system in spite of it being declared illegal is probably the greatest stain on the country's conscience. The attitudes and behaviour of those that still believe in, and practise, the system's precepts are, by any standards, shocking and deeply repulsive. The failure to root out this system seems to lie in self-interest and unjust prerogatives, with people benefiting from the system clutching on to it for psychological security and because it provides them easy victims and scapegoats – the members of the lower castes.

However, there have been concentrated efforts to rid society of this disease, and one such effort is a remarkable boarding school in South India where children of all castes and from different walks of life live and are taught together. In that school – reputed to be the best in the country – no consideration is given to parents' economic status, social standing, or caste; and the students themselves often become the catalysts for change in the attitudes of their parents and other relatives.

In India astonishing extremes of contrasts and contradictions are noticeable everywhere, and it is not uncommon to catch a glimpse of radiant holiness in the midst of shocking violence, both verbal and physical; dismal poverty and starvation amid scandalous displays of wealth; sublime beauty – both natural and human – and disturbing ugliness; genuine compassion and scandalous exploitation; brilliant displays of intelligence and widespread ignorance and illiteracy. India is a functioning democracy and, yet, here there is also institutionalized inequality, and female selflessness and commitment often have to do daily battle with entrenched male chauvinism. And while it has changed and progressed much over the course of the last three decades, there remains much to be done, especially with regards to its social development. Blindly following of the West and adopting its values will only lead to more problems in the future; India must find its own enlightened path for itself to follow.

Spiritually, I owe a lot to India, and here I take the opportunity to acknowledge my huge debt to a few remarkable Indians, from Krishnamurti, to Padre Aaron, Chhanda Bose, Dr. Nalini, Vivekananda, and many forgotten others. They have all given me hope and reasons to believe that a better world is indeed still a possibility.

Bangladesh 1: migthy rivers

Bangladesh 2: dangerous infrastructures

Bangladesh 3: river traffic

Bangladesh 4: river tourism boat

Africa 1: rudimentary poultry transport

Africa 2: rural classroom

Tanzania 1: rural family

Tanzania 2: literacy class

Africa : school under a tree

Gambia 1: illiterate children

Gambia 2: adult education

Gambia 3: open air teaching

Gambia 3: village people

Gambia 4: looking for food

Gambia 5: the Gambian river

Africa: Grandpa and Grandson

Massai of Tanzania

African female group

Cambodia 1: rural primary school kids

Bangladesh street children

The author in Africa

Rural children in Asia

Part III

THE FOREIGN AID CIRCUS

21

THIRD WORLD DEVELOPMENT, FIRST WORLD FAILURE

At the beginning of the 21st century, about fifty percent of the population of Bangladesh – approximately 150 million people – was illiterate. In order to alleviate the problem the government had set up a new and separate department – the Department of Mass Education – and asked for financial and technical assistance from foreign donors. Eight bilateral and multilateral agencies responded, providing close to a billion American dollars as funds for the massive government-led and controlled Non-formal Education (NFE) campaign. However, at no time was the government of Bangladesh or any of its partners in the vast and overambitious project – NGOs, bilateral donors, multilateral international agencies, regional authorities, local communities, and ultimate beneficiaries – in a position to absorb effectively and constructively such a great amount of funds. And yet, in the middle of all the confusion, the head of the World Bank in Washington urged the Prime Minister of Bangladesh to accept another 120 million dollars in low interest loans already earmarked for the same project. And against the recommendations from her advisers not to accept such an untimely offer, as it would not only contribute to an increase in the country's debt and be of no practical use because of lack of adequate absorption capacity, the greedy and incompetent Prime Minister accepted it. The implications of such an inappropriate and undemocratic decision by the highest political authority of the land were clear: growing dependency of the country on foreign funds; increasing corruption at the highest levels; heavier debts to service and repay over a longer period of time, which entailed a heavier financial burden on the country's youth and future generations. All of this, simply because the World Bank wanted to disburse its arbitrarily earmarked funds in order to obtain more at a later stage, regardless of the impact of its ill-advised move on Bangladesh and its already struggling populations.

Ten years later, the NFE programme has proven a disappointment, with in-depth analyses showing that the factors behind its failures have been the same as those behind similar programmes in other parts of the world: namely, lack of a clear and realizable long-term vision and coherent policies on learning, its purpose, objectives and strategies; over centralized decision making process, financial management, and content definition; poor coordination between actors and stakeholders at all levels, including within the donor group; faulty planning, monitoring and evaluation; absence of political will, and transparency and accountability, especially at national level; damaging corruption (between 1999 and 2002, Bangladesh had been declared the most corrupt country in the world by Transparency International, and the Ministry of Education the most corrupt ministry within the country); gross incompetence and dishonesty, with the behaviour and approach of donors often as much a problem as the attitude of the country's highest authorities. Instead of benefiting its target population, the programme has served to enrich further the political and bureaucratic elites, who have schemed and interfered their way to help themselves to the donors' largesse. The donors, meanwhile, in their naiveté, not only failed to face the scourge of corruption and incompetence but were also guilty of imposing Western approaches on an ill-prepared population.

A Nordic country providing assistance to Bangladesh in the field of mass education in the nineties was informed by its own international consultant – who had been working for four years in the field – that large chunks of the sixty million dollars that had been invested into the multi-donor programme had been grossly misused and officers of the Bangladeshi government had diverted funds for their own personal use. However, even after being given significant details of the embezzlement, the Nordic country's government decided to do nothing about it. The reason given to the utterly bewildered consultant was thus: if the Nordic country were to stop its current funding another rich country's aid agency would take over and replace them and the corruption would continue. Such unwillingness on the part of a respected donor to stop the rot is symptomatic of the way in which foreign aid funds often support and encourage the corrupt practices of the elites, much to the detriment of the supposed beneficiaries.

In Gambia, donors in the nineties convinced the government that strengthening the existing but weak Western type educational system was an absolute priority for the country. With massive technical and financial assistance from donors more schools were built, even in remote areas; teachers and administrators were recruited and trained; furniture, books and equipment were purchased; new curricula were devised and introduced. A reinforced education system was rapidly implemented in a top down manner on passive and, at times, reluctant recipients with little local consultation and participation. In remote parts of the country, some ethnic minorities strongly resisted the implementation of the programme by refusing to send their children to the "white man's school". The tribal elders and parents believed that the schools made the children – especially girls – bad, and transformed their mentality and caused them to be alienated from their own culture and traditions; they feared an eventual loss of both their identity and their children.

The programme, needless to say, was a failure, and the cause of the failure was the absence of negotiations with the community and a failure to ensure their participation; the ignorance of donors and the government of local needs and aspirations; and the imposition in a top down manner of an ill designed programme. And yet, it would have been relatively easy to solve the problem by aligning the programmes to suit the needs of the communities, as local Koranic schools successfully do, even though they too face serious problems, including the exploitation and abuse of children.

In another part of West Africa, a vocational training project designed to contribute to the training of unemployed and unskilled youngsters was set up and implemented by a multilateral agency. Some years later, the agency recruited an external consultant to evaluate the impact of the ongoing project. The results of were catastrophic: most trained youngsters did not find jobs and were even more frustrated than before.

Again, failure to design programmes in line with, and relevant to, local needs and opportunities led to growing disillusionment and resentment among the youth, and this threatened the fragile stability of the few villages where the project was being implemented. The evaluation report analysed the reasons for failure and proposed a series of recommendations and measures that would, if implemented, have transformed the programme into a powerful instrument of rural development and self-reliance. However, months later, the evaluator got hold of the report after it had been edited by the agency's headquarters. The report was unrecognisable – negative findings had been eliminated and replaced by fanciful positive results, and most of the original recommendations had been either removed from the report or transformed to correspond to the dreamt-up findings. A second phase of the project – a carbon copy of the first – had been recommended, contrary to the original report, which had suggested that there should not be a second phase unless the project, its objectives, contents, approach, and overall strategy were comprehensively revised until they were in line with the original recommendations. The external agency's desire to obtain fresh funds so as to provide continued employment to both agency personnel and external consultants, of course, had taken precedence over the painful necessity of improving the design of the faulty project.

In the nineties, the Ministry of Labour in Cambodia requested financial and technical assistance in setting up a large and multi-objective countrywide vocational training project. A team comprising six international consultants and an equal number of local counterparts was set up to implement the project. The team leader was an incompetent and quite devious Indian gentleman who had been recruited by the Khmer project director on the basis of a discreet arrangement between the two which entailed the team leader relinquishing a part of his monthly salary to the equally incompetent and corrupt project director. Progress reports were circulated every third month by the team leader. The purpose of the reports was to provide all stakeholders information regarding the progress in the implementation of the project. Over the course of a year, four such reports were produced. However, comparing their contents it was obvious that the only part of the reports that had changed was the date of their publication as listed on the front page!

And in the Philippines, not very long ago, there was a practice of creaming off a percentage of all remittances sent to the country by the millions of Filipinos who work abroad, with the president and her immediate entourage being the sole beneficiaries. This practice was revealed by a staff member of the World Bank, whose leadership must surely have been as aware of the same, and yet chose to remain silent on the issue, perhaps to preserve the bank's relationship with the president.

In Nepal, years of foreign assistance in a wide variety of fields has done little to help the country and raise the living standards of the population. In the late eighties, Kathmandu, the capital, was a very liveable, and even pleasant, city, with charming green suburbs and paddy fields ringed by a stunning view of the snow-covered Himalayas; the pollution was bearable and the electricity supply reliable. Today, much of these have disappeared and pollution is everywhere, and the city itself is overcrowded and dangerous; greenery is hard to find and electricity can be unavailable for as many as eighteen hours a day. Politically the nation is increasingly divided and conflicts between ethnic groups are on the rise; poverty is rampant and ever increasing, while transport and communication infrastructure are often non-existent; health and education systems remain inadequate and often inaccessible; and unemployment, especially among the youth, is widespread, forcing many to migrate abroad in search of work.

Many Nepalis, especially intellectuals, have begun to question the cosy arrangements between the Kathmandu based governing class and donors, especially given the fact that despite massive amounts of aid, the country has not progressed over the last twenty years. They have also begun to question donors on their responsibilities, and efforts have been made to hold them accountable to a degree for the utter mess the country is in today.

Alas, Nepal is a typical case of a largely failed state; and such failure, it seems, is both the result of the incompetence, lack of vision, and absence of political will of successive national governments; and the blind support, and even connivance, of donors to inadequate government priorities and policies and strategies. It is also a result of the imposition of their own pet programmes and projects on passive recipients. It is fair to say that at this stage of Nepal's development foreign aid in the country has as a whole been more hindrance than a help in its attempts at improving the basic living conditions of its downtrodden masses. As in many other countries, foreign aid in Nepal has over the years contributed to the passivity and dependence of successive governments while also sapping people's inner drive and their capacity to become lastingly self-reliant.

In Cambodia the rebuilding of a functioning formal educational system has taken years, and will probably take several generations to complete, if at all it is completed. The project has been plagued by donor intrusion and infighting, along with corruption and incompetence at the leadership levels, and a lack of community involvement. The average salary of a teacher in Cambodia is sixty US dollars a month, and they often have to take up second and third jobs so as to make ends meet. As a result, absenteeism among teachers is high across the country and commitment and motivation low, and the unwillingness of the government and donors to respond to the needs and aspirations of the population do not bode well for the future of education in the country.

In Nepal, the education and training systems suffer from severe limitations due to the country's terrain and the resulting isolation of many of its villages, extreme poverty, poor infrastructure, widespread government corruption and incompetence, and frequent socio-political upheavals. Added to that, is the fact that the country is composed of a multiplicity of ethnic groups, all with different histories, cultures, languages, and learning needs. There is a need for a fundamental re-evaluation and transformation of formal education here so as to better respond to the real educational needs of the population. The expensive and mostly Western type of school system in vogue is particularly ill suited – culturally, socially and economically – to a mostly rural population. However, ignoring this situation, national authorities – supported by a host of donors – seem to continue to assume that superficial adjustments to a policy that involves building more schools, devising and imposing academically oriented programmes and recruiting and training teachers from the centre will progressively solve the many issues plaguing the educational sector. What is needed in Nepal is a decentralization of policy formulation, decision making, and financing; along with empowerment of local communities, teachers and parents; because an educational system is only successful when the responsibility is shared between all stakeholders and not just that of a few specialists.

The combination of factors that account for the regular failure of development programmes are largely the same across the world. Failure, more often than not, is first and foremost the result of human error and incompetence, especially at central level. Added to that is a lack of long term vision; absence of clear and realistic policies; overambitious objectives and inappropriate strategies; insufficient political will and lack of political commitment; grossly ignorant, incompetent, and indifferent decision makers; irrelevant programme content, and ineffective methodologies and approaches. Further, this situation is frequently compounded by a lack of transparency and accountability on the part of politicians and bureaucrats, and their own greed and self-centredness.

Also, external actors – such as donors, bilateral and multilateral agencies, etc. – at times further complicate matters by accepting without question short-sighted policies and flawed programme designs and objectives. As has been seen earlier, the inability to tailor programmes to the needs of beneficiaries, and the unwillingness of decision makers to let target individuals and communities play an essential role in key aspects of the programme seriously jeopardize the usefulness and impact of the programme.

The few examples above represent only a tiny fraction of many instances of avoidable failures in countries where foreign assistance is an integral part of the economy. Not surprisingly, key actors working within this vast and lucrative sector – especially for highly paid foreign consultants – very rarely, if ever, openly talk about and discuss such instances of failure. An absence of honest self-questioning and a culture of silence help explain to an extent the many failures of foreign aid, especially the fact that an instrument meant to promote human betterment, socio-economic development, and national progress is far too often transformed into a serious obstacle for the target nation/ population to transcend.

The donors' ignorance, arrogance, and hypocrisy all too often combine with the recipient leadership's greed, incompetence, and indifference, and this results in denying millions of destitute people the huge potentials that lie latent in a balanced and committed partnership between the two. Foreign aid all too often provides useful measures to contribute only to a decrease in high unemployment rates in rich Western countries; it also provides ego boosting escapes to qualified foreigners who are non entities in their own country but who see their own social status and finances dramatically improve while working in a developing country. Western assistance is a double-edged sword which under the pretext of assisting the poor often pursues other – more selfish – goals; the creation of new markets and trade opportunities being one; another being to increase the importance and influence of the donor country so as to have access to opportunities and benefits in the recipient country. True compassion and genuine commitment to the poor are very rarely in the minds of donors, and the business of foreign aid is run for the most part by bureaucrats who value efficiency over empathy, performance over human emotions, and delivery rates over understanding.

Most economically depressed and politically unstable countries that request assistance from rich, developed nations are often those that have suffered the ravages of colonialism and slavery. This goes to explain to a degree the persistence of underdevelopment in many African and Asian countries. Of most significance is the fact that colonial powers imposed not just arbitrary divisions and boundaries, often ignoring and cutting across tribal and ethnic boundaries; but also structures such as nation states on ill prepared populations. And the fact is that foreign aid designed – and continues to design – its interventions in terms of these artificially created boundaries rather than focusing their efforts on long existing and cohesive tribal entities and groups, which has led to an obvious reduction in the effectiveness and impact of the proposed assistance.

And, often, independence has not helped matters much, as the ways of the colonialist have been absorbed and copied by those that have inherited power from them and who treat their people much as they themselves had been formerly treated. As during the colonial years, the wide cultural gap between the administration and the population – especially rural communities – persists today. Such a gap cannot be bridged as long as Western trained and city based bureaucrats continue to look down upon the rural population ignorant and incapable of assuming responsibility for their own development and the rural population continue to remain suspicious and fearful of civil servants.

The lasting impact of colonialism and slavery has not been limited to culture, politics, and the economy, but is perhaps most visible in the way colonized populations – even after generations of being emancipated – often judge themselves inferior to their colonizers; and by proxy, politicians and civil servants. This has led to both an undermining of the self-confidence of the dominated population while instilling a sense of superiority and arrogance in those that seek to aid and assist them; as was the case in France, where "la mission civilisatrice de la France en Afrique" used to be talked about openly and with a great degree of condescension. In several ways, foreign aid today is often a veiled and more sophisticated prolongation of the hypocrisies, double standards, greed, and arrogance of colonialism; and this unhealthy development – never quite openly spoken about and often denied – continues despite the empty slogans and platitudes about equal partnership, local ownership, local participation, etc. – ideas that are hardly ever translated to reality.

Over the years very few Europeans have had the courage and willingness to face up to the long lasting ravages inflicted by colonialism and the ongoing failures of foreign aid. Admitting failure is never easy for any individual or society, and this is especially true for developed societies. The West has been, and continues to be, very good at providing easy but dubious explanations for its own failures, and the recipient governments and people are often used as scapegoats in these explanations. Also, the West continues to be highly hypocritical in its dealings with the recipient countries, pretending, on the one hand, to provide assistance out of the goodness of its heart, while often offering only tied aid – i.e. aid subject to certain conditions; for instance, obligation to purchase equipment and use consultants from the donor country only, and applying double standards that serve to profit the donor country more than the downtrodden populations of the recipient. This has often been used as an instrument to manipulate and subjugate governments and people as well as promote Western commercial interests.

The donor/recipient relationship has always been a deeply flawed and one sided affair where the one who gives is also the one who makes all the decisions; decisions that often favour the donor rather than the recipient. Added to this is the recipient's frequent diffidence and reluctance to state their own opinions firmly for fear of upsetting donors and jeopardizing access to funds.

22

DONOR INFLEXIBILITY AND OTHER LESSONS FROM THE FIELD

As has been stated many times before, foreign aid policies conceived in economically advanced Western capitals often lack a sound and in-depth understanding of the needs, constraints, capacities, and aspirations of the ultimate beneficiaries, and is often based on simplistic and unproven assumptions. Such policies are often seen by aid recipients as arrogant and condescending and their implementation can create exaggerated expectations which often lead to resentment.

Also, the use of highly paid and privileged international consultants, rather than contributing to solving local difficulties, often creates problems of its own. Cultural and wealth differences between beneficiaries and consultants often prevent the establishment of genuine cooperation and constructive dialogues, and in some cases foreign consultants are perceived as aloof talkers and controllers, or even agents of neo-colonialist enterprises.

The aftermath of the genocide in Rwanda in April 1994 offers a good example of this kind of situation. Following the influx of millions of Tutsi refugees into the Kagera region of Northern Tanzania, swarms of aid workers – primarily from the UN refugee agency, UNHCR – arrived in the region to provide emergency assistance and relief. The situation of these well paid and superbly equipped international aid workers was completely in contrast with the destitute Tanzanians of the region and was the cause of serious tensions. Also, the arrival of aid workers resulted in a drastic increase in market prices, such that it forced the locals to leave the region and resettle elsewhere

The recent introduction of new approaches – such as decentralization, local ownership, partnership of equals, popular participation, local empowerment, etc. – at times seem to exist only to make donors and their centrally devised policies more palatable to locals, who are usually well aware of their powerlessness and of the fact that the one with the money makes all the decisions and the only way to ensure continued access to funding is silence and acceptance.

Increasingly aware of the fact that the use of international consultants for technical assistance purposes is costly and often counterproductive, recipient governments have begun to request the recruitment of much cheaper national consultants, as they are more knowledgeable about local cultures. However, they often have few relevant skills and are more easily manipulated by the national governments who employ them. Also, as direct foreign financial assistance regularly contributes to corruption, especially at the highest levels of recipient countries, channelling funds through NGOs rather than through ministries is one of the preferred alternatives. However, this practice is not without its problems. Often, NGOs are run by those near to ministers and high level bureaucrats, and their sole purpose is to access available donor funds.

In light of numerous failures worldwide, the project approach to development has become increasingly inadequate and is now being abandoned by some donors. Projects are usually time bound and implement top down and inflexible Western practices and approaches. Such practices are often alien to locals and they cannot understand them. Moreover, projects are often poorly designed by hard pressed foreign consultants lacking both time and an understanding of local needs. The belief that foreigners – no matter how qualified – are better at analysing the needs of local problems is an erroneous and dangerous assumption that must be abandoned in favour of partnerships between equals – local population and external agents. This shift obviously requires major mentality changes, especially on the part of foreigners. Year after year lip service is paid to concepts such as capacity building through training, etc.; but proposed projects and programmes rarely offer structures and funding that support the regular training and retraining of beneficiaries and field workers, who when external consultants leave are often incapable of taking over and assuming responsibilities for the transformation of a time limited project into a permanent and sustainable programme or institution.

In the education sector, centrally designed projects and programmes often fail to take into account regional and local realities, conditions, and the essential training and learning needs of concerned groups. Often, education and vocational training are limited to providing knowledge and skills that are irrelevant to local contexts and labour markets, and they serve, instead, to strengthen the capacities of local elites and bureaucrats at the expense of poorer and less visible and less assertive members of society, especially minorities. The importance and role of teachers within the overall educational process is often overlooked, as is the crucial importance of a long term vision and relevant policies patiently elaborated with the active involvement of all concerned, including rural communities.

There is often also a serious level of ignorance and lack of concern on the part of government officers when it comes to the spending of loan/grant money. Sometimes, poorly informed government officials are ignorant of the fact that loans – so often wasted – will need to be repaid by future generations. Also, local communities are frequently sidelined by government officials. Unless this changes, and the ultimate beneficiaries are brought to the centre of the decision making process, development will fail.

23

AID THAT WORKS

Although much of what passes for foreign aid is currently too often more an obstacle to development than a support to it, there are, fortunately, examples of aid that work and that have helped people become self-reliant rather than increasing their dependence and helplessness. Unfortunately, however, examples of positive and successful aid hardly ever emerge out of the assistance that is provided by donor governments to recipient governments. One of the main reasons for this appears to be the fact that government to government aid is too often treated as yet another administrative exercise between two or more bureaucracies, rather than as a matter of grave human necessity. Administrative considerations take precedence and objectives are decided upon, strategies designed, and progress measured by the fulfilment of largely administrative and financial goals, rather than by the quality and long term impact of activities on ultimate beneficiaries.

Small scale projects or programmes set up and jointly run by NGOs, both local and international, and associations – for instance, women's groups from both developed and developing nations – with active local participation tend to produce more positive and lasting results than large and ambitious top down programmes meant to impress and show off the donor's activities. The quality of relationships between recipients and donors in the case of small scale non-governmental interventions are often more balanced and constructive; they tend to look for and support local initiatives, encourage local involvement, and take into account local needs and build upon locally available capacities and facilities. There are numerous examples across the developing world of small scale programmes that have succeeded and brought lasting relief as well as new opportunities to beneficiaries; of these I have chosen to illustrate the following:

The Rishi Valley Educational Centre (RVEC) in South India is an example of a locally developed multidimensional educational programme that is not time bound; that regularly learns from past mistakes; and that constantly tries to expand and improve its objectives, strategies, activities, and long term impact. The RVEC is a tangible demonstration of the fact that learning can be a powerful and lasting source of joy, fulfilment, and human transformation; as well as an effective tool for poverty reduction and self-reliance.

The factors behind the success of the RVEC are active local participation and involvement of ultimate beneficiaries in the key aspects of the programme, especially decision making; mutual respect between donors and recipients, and a willingness to learn from one another, as well as from past mistakes; the capacity of all actors to question every aspect of the programme and a willingness to change course and innovate if and when required; genuine commitment to agreed upon goals on the part of all participants; regular monitoring and evaluation of the programme's progress; and transparency and accountability. These factors help explain the success not only of RVEC but of similar programmes in other parts of the developing world.

A powerful and sound vision of life and learning guides all aspects of Rishi Valley's work, and great emphasis is placed on self-knowledge; the understanding of one's own conditioning; the importance of human relationships; and the need to transcend self-imposed psychological limitations so that latent human capacities for growth, altruism, and self-reliance are developed to the fullest and lead on to the flowering of human goodness and peaceful coexistence.

The staff at the RVEC are unified around this vision, and within the centre there are no hierarchical structures based on caste, qualification, or achievement; instead, the relationship between staff members, as that between staff and students, is marked by a sense of conviviality based on mutual respect and solidarity. Also, local communities – especially parents – are fully involved in all aspects of school life, including administration and decision making.

Although the centre follows national and state syllabuses, it also offers many other options to choose from. The approach to teaching is very different from that used in most public and private schools around the world, in that it starts where the individual is and builds up from there on. The system is flexible enough to adjust and adapt to each child and their learning needs. Each child can move through the programme at their own pace up what is called a ladder of capacities, and results – academic or otherwise – are never compared. Dialogue, praise, and support, rather than criticism, scolding, and denigration are the norms, and the relationship between student and teacher is founded on genuine care and on the principle that students and teachers both learn from each other. The end result is joyful students, contended teachers, and satisfied parents.

The RVEC has won several international awards for its achievements, especially its methodological successes, and it has not only been declared the best school in India several times but has also become a significant model for other schools worldwide, which is testament to the success of its innovative methods and approach.

The women associations of Senegal and Burkina Faso represent another example of successful learning programmes combining formal, informal, and non formal educational approaches at grass roots level. Both programmes run over several years without time limitations and bureaucratic constraints, and are an example of how illiterate rural women when united for the purpose of improving living conditions can be an incredible and unstoppable force.

Despite the interference of their jealous and fearful men, lack of governmental support, and many obstacles, the women in both countries were able to dramatically improve their economic situation, increase their political power, and steadily move towards greater independence, not only from their men but also from the government. The success of the programmes can be attributed almost entirely to the women, although intelligent external support and guidance – primarily from mature and experienced NGOs – did play a part. The end result was a drop in child mortality, better health practices, increased democracy, and a decrease in discrimination.

One of the key factors behind the success of the programmes was the availability of functional literacy training along with skills training in occupations associated with women – such as gardening, animal husbandry, tailoring, etc; which are illustrative of how things as simple as basic market related training, supported where necessary by modest loans and technical guidance, can rapidly and cheaply change the lives of the poor and illiterate.

And this kind of thinking has led to the success in Thailand of the countrywide Non Formal Education (NFE) countrywide programme, which has become a model for other South East Asian countries to follow. Here, functional literacy is directly linked to skills training and occupations, meaning that what is being taught is immediately usable at work by beneficiaries. Local circumstances, locally available resources, materials, and facilities are taken into account during programme design, thus lowering costs. The skills necessary for the beneficiaries – for instance, in the case of a carpenter, the ability to read instructions, measure, record figures, manage accounts, etc.– are analysed and programme content is built around this analysis. Trainers and teachers are recruited and trained locally, thus increasing their acceptability and support by villagers. Local communities are fully involved in the programme and both participate in it as well as support it by contributing funds, building material, labour, etc. Obstacles and challenges are overcome through dialogue and negotiations between concerned stakeholders and no potential solution is imposed from above. As such, local communities and recipients identify with and cherish the programme, which is theirs rather than the government's or some other external entity's, and most people completing the courses do usually find work with an employer or become confident enough to engage in their own business.

Meanwhile, in Bangladesh, BRAC – the world's largest NGO, and certainly one of its most successful – works closely with grass-roots groups whose initiatives they support. Focusing primarily on women, BRAC's non-formal education programme offers access to literacy and market related training to millions of poor Bangladeshis. The success of the programme, in contrast to the dismal failure of the government's NFE programme, is due to the adherence to, and the application of, a few crucial rules; such as, investigating, understanding, and taking into account local cultures in setting up programmes; carrying out in-depth surveys and analysis of the needs, aspirations, and capacities of future beneficiaries, and taking these results into account in programme formulation; ensuring collective involvement and participatory decision making at local level; searching for, encouraging, and supporting local initiatives, and never imposing externally devised ready made programmes; relying on sound planning and implementation; conducting monitoring and participatory evaluation of all programmes with the help of representatives of all concerned stakeholders; using local resources – human and material – whenever possible; demanding total transparency and accountability at all levels and in all components of the programme.

Some years ago, an isolated and grossly neglected ethnic minority group in Northern Cambodia requested the assistance of an international NGO in setting up a rudimentary primary school for the children of a number of local communities. The biggest problem was regarding the language of instruction to be used in the school, since both the children and their parents had no language other than their native tongue, while one of the Ministry of Education's most stringent rules was that all Cambodian children regardless of ethnicity had to be schooled in Khmer. The NGO and the concerned villages came up with an elegant solution, which the ministry accepted. For the first year or two, the children were allowed to speak and be instructed in their own language while learning Khmer at the same time. As a result, drop-out and absentee rates among both teachers and pupils fell immediately and the overall academic performance improved dramatically. Parents, children, and teachers all became strong supporters of the local school, which not only became a focal point for learning but also an example of the harmonious integration of an ethnic minority into wider Khmer society.

24

RETHINKING AND TRANSFORMING AID

When development aid is made available by a country that shares common cultural values, and sometimes a common language, with another close but less developed country, the process is often smoother and more productive. That is, of course, provided there are no serious issues between the concerned countries. History, conflict, political interference, jealousy, and mutual suspicions often make any fruitful cooperation impossible. But when such obstacles are removed via dialogue, then cooperation, sharing, and mutual assistance not only become possible but more fruitful than in the skewed partnerships between developed and developing nations. As such, these partnerships offer more possibilities for cooperation and development than the traditional approach. One of the main reasons for this is historical, in that the burdens of colonialism and Western dominance are no longer at play. Given the possibilities that such partnerships have to offer, the model needs to be seriously studied as a possible solution to the problems currently plaguing the development – in particular the foreign aid – sector.

However, partnership between developing nations is not the only solution for an effective aid policy, and aid – which ought to be renamed mutual cooperation – can work well provided that all involved actors at every level of the sector begin to question and revise the assumptions and attitudes that have long governed their practice and approach. The same actors must also learn from past mistakes and make sure they never lose sight of the ultimate goal – the welfare of the beneficiaries. Also, true partnership and balanced and equitable collaboration and participation must become guiding principles, and beneficiaries must be treated with greater respect and dignity, so that they have the confidence to become the ultimate decisions makers and participate in all phases of the programme, from design to implementation.

Moreover, government to government assistance must be progressively abandoned in favour of direct assistance to the people, via NGOs and organized groups if necessary; and programmes must be guided by a clearly stated and all-encompassing vision, targets, and objectives, all of which must be regularly evaluated and adapted as necessary. Also, programmes must be designed according to the outcome of necessary analyses and studies regarding the needs and aspirations – both current and future – of the beneficiaries, and programme content designed to represent practical and relevant responses to the same. Programme facilitators, too, must be selected not in terms of mere academic qualifications, but on this very important criterion – empathy. All measures must be taken to ensure that they are familiar with the needs of their targets, are properly trained, have regular access to training and support, are properly treated, and are adequately rewarded for their efforts.

Part IV

The Old World and the New

25

SWITZERLAND TODAY

In the years immediately following the end of the Second World War a wave of hope swept across Europe, and in Switzerland, which had escaped the ravages of war, these years were when this small alpine country began to establish the base upon which its formidable economy would later grow. However, not all Swiss people benefited from this surge of economic growth, which was built on cheap foreign labour and dubious foreign investments.

The fact that Switzerland had not been involved in the war and the influence of a widespread Calvinistic (and Lutheran) work ethic combined with a democratic type of decentralization functioning, a central location, excellent planning and organizational skills, as well as sheer luck and cunning were major factors in the nation's steady economic and political success. Such success, however, has over the years led to increased smugness and arrogance, especially among bankers and heads of major multinational corporations, whose business is cloaked in secrecy and marked by a lack of scruples and accountability. Moreover, the timidity of the Swiss government – who have often been described as lackeys – has allowed the same bankers and corporations to function without check. This, of course, has led to a serious dent in the reputation of the country as a clean, neutral, and idyllic land; the land of Heidi, milk, chocolate, cheese, and cuckoo clocks. Instead, it has turned –to paraphrase the words of the Economist – into a land growing fatter and richer on the backs of other people; a land, as some have remarked, which is a prison where the guards are its own citizens; a land – as Max Frisch pointed out – which is surprised to discover that the migrant workers which drives its economy are humans and not mere cogs in the compassion-less machine that is the Swiss economy.

Economic success has drastically transformed traditional values and social realities, and not always for the better. Growing prosperity has encouraged the emergence of excessive individualism, greed, and inequality, while progressively weakening all sense of solidarity and cooperation. The excessive materialism and obsession with organizational efficiency and competition have led to a dehumanization of relationships to the extent that life itself has become a meaningless affair; an exercise in survival, itself a vicious cycle from which many struggle to break free via illusory forms of escape – entertainment, sport, sex ... – while pursuit of lasting happiness and the sense of spirituality which gives meaning to one's life seems to have been either relegated to the to-do list for old age or simply forgotten.

Amid all this hankering after prosperity and the focus on economic success over all else, a few essential questions remains unasked: Will this be worth it, in the long run? Should we – the Swiss – rejoice in living in a sheltered and sterile Eldorado without concern for our responsibility to the wider world? Or should we not begin to ask serious questions about our role in the world?

The Swiss have much to contribute to the world and have the resources to transform it for the better. However, there is no motivation to do so, and unless a major transformation occurs in their own thinking it is likely to remain thus. The fact that in Switzerland rape is frequently considered a minor offence and only lightly punished while economic theft carries hefty sentences is an indicator of how skewed the Swiss value system has become.

My relationship with my country of birth had never been smooth, and I have always felt a sense of discomfort when confronted with the hypocrisy and petty sense of superiority that seems to be the defining character trait of the Swiss today. I also feel particularly disturbed by the blind devotion to profit at all cost – especially in the banking, pharmaceutical, and food industries – and in particular when this behaviour has led to wide-scale suffering. For example, the scandalously rich pharmaceutical industry is reluctant to develop remedies for malaria – a disease that kills thousands every year – because the disease is primarily confined to poor Africans who will not be able to afford the medicines. Also, a food giant has been involved in manipulating desperate African mothers by convincing them that powder milk was better for their children than breast milk. Meanwhile, the conduct of Swiss banks in dealing with Nazi Germany and Apartheid South Africa should be a source of national shame; however, this is a nation that is concerned more with a person's fortune than their integrity, as shown by the example of the local mayor who refused to commemorate one of the world's greatest philosophers – who had taught freely in his village for twenty-five years – because his presence had not resulted in any financial benefits!

However, I do have great affection for the Swiss landscape, for the mountains and the many lakes. And I also remember fondly the migrant workers that have helped build the country – the Italians singing while they lunched on salami and Chianti by the Rhine; the Portugese waitresses offering their warm smiles to blasé local burghers; the dedicated Filipino nurses looking after the elderly for a pittance; the many refugees trying hard to rebuild their lives. Alas, a growing proportion of the Swiss population have set themselves firmly against the influx of foreigners, and this despite the fact that they are essential to continued economic growth. The truth is that immigrant workers contribute more to the country than they take from it, and the country is dependent to a large degree on skilled foreign labour: for example, in the hospitals, foreigners now comprise most of the staff.

I have also always been impressed by the way the country's highly decentralized political system functions so smoothly; as I have by its entrepreneurial spirit; its capacity to innovate; to bounce back after setbacks; and its ability to manage challenges through dialogue rather than conflict.

26

NEW ZEALAND – A MODEL STATE?

Much in contrast to Switzerland New Zealand is, in many ways, a model country for the developing world. While a modern and developed country, it nonetheless shares many historical characteristics with countries in the developing world, especially those that have formerly been colonies. A multi-cultural society that has over two centuries experimented with various forms of political and social structures, it has developed remarkably sound institutions and value systems.

Until a few decades ago New Zealand was still largely in thrall to the United Kingdom, which remains the mother country in many of its people's hearts. As is the case with many developing countries, it has suffered the pangs of breaking away from the colonizer and forging its own identity. Additionally, its history as an independent country and its emergence as a developed nation offer many examples of a peaceful and equitable integration of ethnic minorities, immigrants, and women. It is also the country where, over fifty years ago, one of the most sophisticated and fairest social welfare systems in the world was developed. By then equality between the sexes had been a reality for years – New Zealand was the first nation to extend voting rights to women; and migrants – most of them from Europe – were made very welcome and integrated into a friendly and caring society; and it could then boast of one of the world's best education systems. In the fifties and the sixties no other society was as free, safe, and fair as New Zealand. It was then truly classless and offered almost limitless opportunities to locals and immigrants alike.

Several events over the decades have contributed to New Zealand growing out of its dependence on the United Kingdom and the West and asserting its own identity. The first jolt came in the seventies when the UK joined the European Union and abandoned New Zealand, which was much dependent upon British markets for its exports. This was followed by the French nuclear tests in neighbouring Polynesia in the eighties, and the sinking by French intelligence of the Greenpeace ship – The Rainbow Warrior – at Auckland Harbour, both of which led to serious diplomatic crises between the two nations. Emerging from these crises more assertive and confident, the country went through a dramatic economic transformation in the eighties. Government subsidies to farmers were withdrawn, even though this led, initially, to havoc among the farming community, the mainstay of the economy. However, in a remarkable display of resilience and ingenuity, the agricultural sector quickly recovered, but the deeply anchored dependence on the state had to be abandoned.

Today, New Zealand has fashioned an identity for itself and has also become a proud, self-assured, and successful modern nation. However, this process of modernization has not been without its ills, and the country is no more as classless and open as it was in the past. As with all developed countries, greed and materialism have largely replaced equal opportunity and fairness in the value system, especially in urban milieus. This has led to social stratification, growing inequality, and the marginalization of some minorities.

Auckland, the commercial capital of the country, where close to fifty percent of the country's population live and work, has become a sprawling metropolitan centre defined by materialism and brutal competition. And like most Western cities today, it has its slums, its poor and downtrodden – comprising chiefly of migrant workers and ethnic minorities – as well as its uncouth and pompous nouveaux riches flaunting their wealth. Here, tensions between minorities seem to be exacerbated by wide cultural and economic differences and insufficient communication between ethnic groups, as well as by ignorance and prejudice. A significant proportion of the Maori population feel disenfranchised and tensions between New Zealanders of European descent and Maoris over land use, etc. have begun to flare up.

Modern means of transport and the internet have largely helped New Zealand overcome the disadvantages of distance and geographic isolation, and tourism has become a mainstay of the New Zealand economy. However, in many ways, New Zealand's economy is still overly dependent on agriculture and on the whims of other countries and foreign corporations. Australia has a big stake in the economy and, much like the United Kingdom in the seventies, plays an important role in the formulation of economic policies, as well as in decision making. This has led to growing short-termism in the formulation of economic policies, and also to a rather high rate of unemployment, especially among the young. Additionally, unattractive salaries and poor career prospects push many of the youth to leave the country, especially for Australia, where prospects are far more attractive.

Taking into account, then, this progressive deterioration which characterizes many aspects of New Zealand society, can we still consider the country to be a sort of a model society? The answer is complex, as New Zealand has even now not lost all of the characteristics that made it the envy of much of the world, and so as not to be irremediably lost it must again find these qualities and develop them anew. The country has much to offer the world, especially its smaller neighbours in the South Pacific, which benefit a lot already from the generosity and the know how of their larger island neighbour.

Among New Zealand's major assets are the fast growing diversity of its population; intelligent welfare and immigration policies; and a free and fair education system; and to preserve these and counteract the negative effects of self-centred politics and unbridled consumerism, the attitudes and performance of those in positions of power and privilege must be regularly examined and where necessary sanctioned, as they are in a position to dictate the direction of society and the country, and as is the case in most countries they are all too easily influenced by business and financial interests.

Part V

REFLECTIONS

27

LEARNING FROM EACH OTHER

Over the course of a long and often tumultuous journey across four continents I have been particularly blessed and have encountered numerous cultures, peoples, and ways of life, all of which have been a source of enrichment for me. These societies, so very different from our own, are, for the most part, locked in a permanent struggle for survival; and yet there is an emotional warmth in their dealings with each other and also with outsiders that is all too absent in the modern West, where excessively organized social structures often result in stunting the emotional potentials of children and adults alike.

Western learning systems – largely products of the Industrial Revolution – tend to place excessive emphasis on the individual's academic achievements at the expense of a more holistic development that allow for the greater flourishing of potential and natural intelligence. It is quite obvious that the two pursuits – academic excellence and human development – can and ought to go hand in hand and complement each other in order to develop more emotionally balanced and tolerant human beings; however, in formal schools today, children rarely ever have an opportunity to explore themselves and learn about their own emotions. It is unfortunate that the type of education system represented by the formal school has spread across the world and has become the model that most countries, regardless of their capacities, follow. To fulfil their objectives, educational planners and policy makers try to ensure that education systems are framed by proper policies, strategies, goals, etc.; all of which serve to promote and sustain a system based on a limited vision of education. Rarely, if at all, are essential questions about long term effects and consequences and about the quality of pupils asked, and the overall emphasis is on the number of pupils processed by the system. Yet, such questions are absolutely vital to a healthy education system.

Western societies often misunderstand and neglect the needs – including educational needs – of individuals from less privileged backgrounds, of migrants, and of minorities. In failing to do so, they contribute to the emergence and maintenance of class privileges and inequalities. Such situations are, of course, dangerous for society on the whole, as they contribute to increased resentment and anger. Politics, politicians, and bureaucrats are frequently part of the problem, and one cannot hope that politics as it is practised today in many countries – both in the West and in the developing world – can lead to a better world. The very nature of politics, which is concerned solely with winning elections and remaining in power, is extremely detrimental to society, and the urge to be a politician is often a reflection of a human shortcoming.

In many countries lacking government-led social welfare arrangements, the family and community – especially women's groups – play active and constructive roles in the care of the sick, the handicapped, and the old. It is often within such groups that sound and ultimately successful initiatives emerge and grow. As we have seen before, the rate of success of locally initiated ideas and programmes largely surpasses that of externally imposed projects, and the reason for this is simple: locally initiated programmes belong to and are managed by highly motivated local people, who have a sense of responsibility towards the project; while externally initiated and implemented projects rarely ever elicit the same kind of commitment and passion. However, traditional structures and arrangements, especially within rural communities, are often a double edge sword that sometimes can be a hindrance to sustainable development. While traditions of solidarity and mutual assistance are powerful tools that contribute much to the welfare of the communities; long held prejudices, superstitions, etc. can represent equally potent obstacles to the same.

Traditionally, European societies have placed too high a value on thinking and intellectual skills as the only instrument at our disposal to guide us on the path to progress. This stance has led to the neglect of other equally vital qualities, such as compassion and solidarity, and contributed to the development of the individualism and arrogance that plagues Western society today. Other civilizations – especially Asian cultures – have placed an equal emphasis on other human capacities and have developed more holistic approaches to living. One of these is Buddhism, a value system and philosophy from which the West can learn a great deal, especially as its methods – particularly meditation, the practice of which encourages the emergence of otherwise latent human capacities – seem to complement modern scientific methods rather than stand in opposition to them.

Today, up to two billion people live on less than two dollars a day in the developing world. Most of them have no access to electricity, drinking water, sanitation, and access to basic health and educational services . Consequently, they suffer from malnutrition, disease, and illiteracy. Female and child mortality rates in these communities are often the highest in the world, and these people live for the most part in slums, where they are often at the mercy of politicians, bureaucrats, warlords, and criminals. And yet, most of us in the West, engrossed as we are in our own lives and petty problems, appear to be utterly indifferent to such hardship and inequalities. And we are amazed when we discover that here, in the midst of such poverty and misery, we find the human spirit at its most resilient, its most resourceful; and that too, especially among the more downtrodden of the population – the women!

Year after year, in Bangladesh, monsoon rains and storms sweep away the precarious shelters of countless poverty stricken families that live on the rapidly shifting islands on mighty rivers. Year after year, the women gather together and rebuild their huts to the best of their abilities. And they do not complain. Not against the weather, nor against the government, who have so neglected them.

And where are the men in all this? They are preoccupied with their male preoccupations – with sex and their ego. In Western societies, where the rule of law is the norm, women are largely protected from the egotistical pursuits and predatory ways of their men; this leaves them free to fulfil their own potentials without being perceived as threats to men. However, in the developing world, particularly in undemocratic societies, women are often grossly discriminated against, physically exploited, and emotionally abused by men, often with the acquiescence of society. And yet again, it is often in these societies, where women are treated as second rate citizens, that female resilience and courage come to the fore, and in many such societies women play the most important role in ensuring the family's survival.

However, the fact is that in these patriarchal societies even mothers tend to believe that boys are more valuable than girls, and as a result of this ignorance, women themselves help perpetuate the cycle of discrimination against their own sex. The few societies that have managed to give women equal opportunities are flourishing today, and it should be the goal of every nation – developed and otherwise – to aspire to the state of the Scandinavian countries, where equality between the sexes have largely been achieved.

Human beings are reservoirs of immense potential, but it seems that the only domain where we are fulfilling this potential is technology. Our psychological selves, however, have barely evolved and are much the same as our cave dwelling ancestors'. Why do we place so much emphasis on having rather than on being? Even when we understand the terrible consequences of our urge to possess more and more – wars, conflicts, human atrocities. It would seem to me that the task at hand is to allow the development of human beings who have the ability to free themselves from the shackles of centuries of conditioning and indoctrination, along with a direct form of democracy, where the people are the final decision makers. Real democracy, beginning at local level, appears to me the best system for human development, as it allows for the creation of learning opportunities that are not only open to all but also encourage active participation and remain fair and equitable. This is the ground upon which to build the future human being – a being defined not by the values so dear to the Western world today – namely greed and rapacity – but by those it seems to have lost, almost completely – compassion, tolerance, solidarity.

Haute Savoie, France
August 2015.

